The History of Aircraft Nose Art

WWI to Today

Jeffrey L. Ethell and Clarence Simonsen

Foulis

Haynes

The nose art cover painting is in reverent memory of Captain Victor J. France and 116 other combat pilots of the 4th Fighter Group in World War II who did not survive to savor final victory.
Donald E. Allen,
crew chief for *Captain France*

A FOULIS Aviation Book

ISBN 0 85429 934 3

This edition first published 1991

© Jeffrey L. Ethell and Clarence Simonsen, 1991

This edition published by:
Haynes Publishing Group
Sparkford, Nr. Yeovil, Somerset
BA22, 7JJ, England

Original edition published in the USA in 1991 by Motorbooks International Publishers & Wholesalers, Inc., 729 Prospect Avenue, Osceola, WI 54020, USA

Printed and bound in Hong Kong

A catalogue record for this book is available from the British Library

Contents

Acknowledgments

A book like *The History of Aircraft Nose Art* is dependent upon the generosity of a vast number of people. Quite simply, it would have been impossible without them. By sheer volume, it would take a chapter to explain how each of these people contributed and it is a pity that listing their names below is all they'll get out of it.

Nevertheless there was a corps of people who went the extra mile without a complaint. For that special effort we thank William J. Addison for opening his extensive album collection, Steve Birdsall for letting us borrow at will from his rich photo archive, Peter M. Bowers for sending several packages of photos, Gilbert C. Burns for digging deep into his 50th FG memorabilia, John M. Campbell for the countless hours in the darkroom making prints and for sending photos from his own archive, James V. Crow for numerous packages from his extensive files, Larry Davis for sending a substantial number of photos while he was working on his own nose art books, Robert S. DeGroat for opening doors to veterans and for uncovering nose

art history, James H. Farmer for giving permission to quote his own extensive historical work and for providing a ton of photos, Peter M. Grosz for opening his vast World War I photo archive for copying, Dan Hagedorn for his selfless work in spotting and pulling photos for copying, George N. Klare for his willingness to write Chapter 1, Don Malko for traveling to conduct interviews and do extensive photo copy work, Charles Martignette for making a special run through his unique art collection, Ernest R. McDowell for unloading his archives on us, E. P. "Lucky" Stevens for opening his fantastic memorabilia collection for copying, Norm Taylor for allowing us to ransack his substantial photo files, Greg VanWyngarden for providing a wealth of World War I photography and Ron Witt for entrusting his extensive collection of Twentieth Air Force negatives for printing.

And, of course, the nose artists themselves were fantastic with their time, giving long interviews and sharing what was left of their wartime art in photos and sketches.

Nose Artists

Donald E. Allen, Howard M. Bacon, Philip S. Brinkman, Arthur De Costa, Thomas E. Dunn, Nicholas H. Fingelly, Jack Gaffney, John Harding, Thomas E. Harritt, David R. Hettema, Leland J. Kessler, Al G. Merkling, James C. Nickloy, Mike Pappas, David T. Roberts, Rusty Restuccia, Robert T. Sand, Harvey A. Shaw, Anthony L. Starcer, Vernon Wilkes.

Veterans

Robert Abresch, Ike Adamson, Carroll R. "Andy" Anderson, Rhodes F. Arnold, Bob Arnold, Hugh T. Atkinson, Clinton F. Ball, H. Baxter, Russell Beach, Glen B. Bowers, Fred Brown, Raymond S. Brown, Johnny A. Butler, Douglas Canning, Edward C. Carr, C. M. Christoff, Forrest S. Clark, Sid Cohen, William B. Colgan, Foley D. Collins, Jr., James A. Conklin, Bill Cook, Lee Warren Doerr, Ian Duncan, Lawrence G. Estep, Jim Everhart, Frank Fernandez, Matthew A. Fritz, Delos Fuller, F. R. Fuller, Howard "Bud" Goebel, Al Goodwin, William H. Greenhalgh, Robert F. Hahn, Arthur I. Hall, Joe Hammer, Richard C. Harris, William

4

N. Hess, Eugene S. "Mule" Holmberg, William M. Horton, Sigurd L. Jensen, Jr., Casey Laskowski, Earl C. Long, Leo W. Lorenzo, J. Charles Macgill, Joe E. Malsberger, Arthur McArthur, Robert C. Mikesh, Carl Mongrue, Claude Murray, Leroy W. "Ted" Newby, William J. O'Donnell, Richard H. Perley, Loy F. Peterson, Paddy Porter, Edward B. Richie, Brian C. Rogers, Clark B. Rollins, Jr., George W. Roof, William E. Scarborough, Clifford H. Schule, James P. Scott, Marc Shook, Joseph B. Sills, Frank C. Shearin, Jr., William J. Skinner, Wy Spalding, Zack P. Stanborough, James A. Struthers, John W. Sutay, Larry G. Taylor, John A. Tellefsen, Frank Tinsdale, Thomas C. Tracy, Byron Trent, Willis E. Tulare, William A. Turner, Harry Tzipowitz, Harry C. Vaughn, Stuart Watson, Richard Wettour, Kenneth D. Williams, Vance "Bud" Yount.

Individuals

William F. Adams, Paul M. Andrews, Reid Stewart Austin, James R. Benson, Jr., David Berry, Bill Bielauskas, Tim Bivens, Steve Blake, Ray Bowden, Robert N. Bredau, Piet Brouwer, Jim Burridge, S. M. Coates, Philip C. Cohan, William R. Cook, Harley Copic, Brian Cox, Tom Davidson, Al Davies, Christopher Davis, Don "Bucky" Dawson, Robert F. Dorr, Stewart P. Evans, William L. Felchner, Alec Fushi, Harry Gann, Terry Gladwell, David Glover, Luther Gore, Norris Graser, Jon Guttman, Joseph G. Handelman, Michael J. Harney, Leif Hellstrom, Carl Hildebrandt, Tom Ivie, Tony Jarvis, Frederick A. Johnsen, Lawrence J. Hickey, John Kern, Gino Kunzle, Henny Kwik, John W. Lambert, Henry A. Lapa, Jr., Michael Leister, Jonathan Lewis, Gus Lerch, Everett S. Lindley, Don Linn, Ron G. Mackay, Bill Marshall, Beall J. Masterson, David W. Menard, Ian Melton, Joe Michaels, Jeff Millstein, Robert Mott, Douglas D. Olson, David R. Osborne, Barry Pattison, Alain Pelletier, Peter Petrick, Barbara Pleasance, Alfred Price, Willi Reibel, Alan Richie, Mark Richie, Bob Rocker, H. W. Rued, Frank F. Smith, Jack H. Smith, Samuel L. Sox, John Stanaway, Hans-Heiri Stapfer, Phil Starcer, John Swearengin, John Szabo, Barrett Tillman, Frank L. Tripodi, Ray Wardell, Bill Wolfinger, Gary M. Valant, Oskar Wagner, Douglas A. Zalud, Gunther Zerhusen.

Organizations

Smithsonian Institution, National Air & Space Museum: Dan Hagedorn, Larry Wilson, Melissa Keiser, Dana Bell. Strategic Air Command: T. Sgt. Alan "Doc" Dockery. Eighth Air Force Historical Society: John H. Woolnough. US Air Force Academy: Duane J. Reed, Robert Troudt. Public Archives of Canada: Carl Vincent. Canadian Government Expositions and Audio Visual Centre, Ottawa. National Museums of Canada: A. J. Shortt. Canadian Forces Photographic Unit: Maj. K. W. Farrell. Canadian War Museum: Dick Malott. Kitchen Sink Press: Doreen Riley. *Esquire* magazine: Eric Perret. American, British and Canadian postal services: sorters and carriers who never lost or damaged a thing. Lockheed Corporation: Eric Schulzinger. Boeing Company: Marilyn A. Phipps. Maryland ANG: Col. Bruce Tuxill. Walt Disney Archives: David R. Smith. *Air Force Times*: Ruth Chandler. *Army Times*: J. William Drach. Eagle Squadron Association: Jim Gray. Memphis Belle Memorial Association: Harry Friedman. Mojave County Historical Society: Norma Hughes. 2nd Air Division Association: David G. Patterson, Francis Di Mola. 4th FG Association: Charles E. Konsler. 20th CMS Association: David C. Ecoff, Sr. 56th FG Association: Leo D. Lester. 307th BG Association: James M. Kendall. 339th FG Association: Harry R. Corey, James R. Starnes. 351st BG Association: Ben Schohan. 355th FG Association: Robert E. Kuhnert. 379th BG Association: Frank L. Betz. 385th BG Association: John C. Ford, Paul R. Schulz. No. 419 Squadron, RCAF: Vincent Elmer. 486th BG Association: Robert Arnold. 494th BG Association: David H. Rogers.

To all of you, our deepest thanks. May the result have been worth your efforts.

Jeff Ethell
Clarence Simonsen

The Future—Research into a subject this broad with such wide appeal never exhausts itself. The authors would be happy to hear from anyone who has more nose art to share with us for possible future volumes and may contact us care of Motorbooks International.

Capt. Ervin C. Ethell, commander of the 39th FS, Johnson Field, Japan, 1949, with his personal F-51D *Jeanie,* named after his wife.

Introduction

The massive resurgence of interest in military aircraft nose art over the past several years has resulted in a plethora of books, magazine articles, and calendars exhibiting this most unique, and on the whole most American, of art forms. Along with this flood has come a drought of analytical and historical research into the subject itself: where it came from, what it meant, those who painted it, why crews wanted it, the aircraft themselves. The list can go on almost indefinitely, since the subject has been so visually exploited and so casually explored.

That was the impetus that drove the authors to produce this first analytical overview of nose art from its beginnings in World War I to its present reappearance on modern military aircraft.

Jeff Ethell's earliest memories of nose art are personal. His father, a USAF squadron commander in the late 1940s, would take him "to work" and he grew up thinking everyone's father had an airfield full of colorfully painted fighters. Erv Ethell's personal P-51D was named *Jeanie* after his wife—Jeff's mom—with a large color portrait under the script lettering on the nose. When Jeff was three years old he would be placed on the wing with this impressive vision of his mother spread before him. The memory has never faded. Through the years as he flew an increasing number of vintage military aircraft and wrote numerous books on aviation history, nose art became a natural part of the process until a sizable collection emerged.

Clarence Simonsen was born in 1944 in Acme, Alberta, Canada, which was a major site for the British Commonwealth Air Training Plan and the emerging postwar Royal Canadian Air Force (RCAF). As a child he watched bright yellow Harvards, at times one after another, cross his farm at zero feet on the local flying instructor's training course. That thunderous sound left a lasting impact on the young lad, who always seemed to be drawing aircraft in his schoolbook margins. In his teens Simonsen had his first exposure to Alberto Vargas and subsequently discovered the impact of this artist's work on World War II nose art.

During his stint in the Canadian Army Simonsen was posted to Cyprus in 1965, the first time he had left Canada, and he wondered if this was how bomber crews felt twenty years earlier. He painted many cartoons for his unit and did his first wall art; he then understood the effect such art had on isolated military men as they came to view it and ask for personal cartoons. By the late 1960s Simonsen was on the Metro Toronto Police Force with his major avocation being the collection of aircraft nose art as an art form. With a major boost from the Eighth Air Force Association and John Woolnough in the 1970s, the Simonsen collection grew by major proportions into one of the most complete of its kind.

The first serious contemplation of nose art appeared in James H. Farmer's *Art and the Airman* series, which ran for several years in the American Aviation Historical Society *Journal*, beginning with the Spring 1973 issue. The premier historian on Hollywood aviation as well as a trained, accomplished artist, Farmer grasped the significance of "a Twentieth Century phase of heraldry or cognizances (in heraldry, the distinguishing crest or other device by which the bearer is recognized), whose traditions go back to the faceless armored European horsemen of the medieval twelfth century [and which] remain today a source of pride in one's self and one's organization." Farmer continued, "As Arthur E. DuBois (WWII's Herald Section Chief, U.S. Army) once observed, 'From such pride (in unit markings) springs discipline; not a discipline born of necessity and fear, but that which is essentially self-discipline, the essence of respect for self, for service, for country.'"

Decorating instruments of war predates recorded history and moves forward: prehistoric clubs, Egyptian chariots, Phoenician war galleys, Spartan shields, Grecian helmets, Roman standards, Viking ships, Zulu regalia, American Indian horses and war paint. The list continues through every culture, revealing what anthropologists and psychologists

MP Clarence Simonsen, Cyprus, mid–1960s, with an example of his early wall art, which inspired him to begin researching the effect of personalized art on military personnel.

have identified as the human need to personalize, trust, and feel affection for those implements which deliver him from or to destruction. Certainly the airplane has become the ultimate example to date, with the possible exception of the space shuttle, which, many argue, still remains an aircraft and is thought of by its crews in the same way.

Medical Corps officers Roy R. Grinkler and John P. Spiegel stated in their 1945 book *War Neuroses* that the US Army Air Forces' (USAAF) mission was "immensely reinforced by the primary love for, and devotion to, aircraft. Planes are loved for their beauty, their performance, and their strength." In 1951 Thomas H.G. Ward wrote an article titled "The Psychological Relationship Between Man and Aircraft" for the *British Journal of Medical Psychology*, developing the point: "When a machine becomes as complicated as an aircraft, with an engine that emits a particular sound, has a particular 'feel' and characteristics and usually a certain amount of beauty, it tends to be regarded somewhat differently. It is looked upon like a living creature having a personality and sometimes even feelings of its own, and this curious animism results in a relationship developing between man and machine which in many ways is similar to relationships that develop between one human being and another human being."

Jim Farmer amplified this by suggesting "man may under certain conditions be in danger of losing an essential part of his own humanity to the machine. We find that many expressions found on impersonal pieces of equipment reveal an effort to personalize or humanize that equipment, and particularly that machine upon which their lives may

depend. Thereby it may be an unconscious attempt to gain mastery of it. As a veteran Vietnam pilot put it: 'I believe that the kind of art we are talking about is deeply related to the very primitive magical notion that, once you have named something you have control over it. Once you name it, you cannot lose any part of yourself to it—you have asserted mastery over it.'"

This "quasi-human personality of an aircraft," remarked Robert N. Bredau in his unpublished master's degree thesis "The Meaning of Nose Art," "is further bolstered by referring to an aircraft with the feminine pronoun 'she' and describing specific handling characteristics with sexual or sensual terms such as 'she flies smooth' or 'she has to be handled carefully,' as described by Ward. Also reflective of the female personalities ascribed to aircraft were the names chosen by air combat crews. Many (but not all) aircraft were named after wives, girlfriends, and mothers."

Judging from the pin-up-inspired nose art of World War II and the Korean War, it is not hard to see why psychologists had a field day. Jim Farmer again: "It has been suggested that one of man's strongest and most persistent fantasies is that of dominance or conquest of the opposite sex. Male mythology supports the belief that 'The idea of being seized and borne off by a ruthless, aggressive male has a universal appeal to the female sex.' We are talking about lustful male conquest; love is not involved, only the assertion of the male belief in his natural dominance." Nothing made war more bearable than the thought of a woman, in both the tenderest and the most degrading forms. Men tend to think most of those things which they cannot have.

In looking through this female-inspired nose art, most has little of love's tender side. Farmer continued: "Indeed [on the whole] there is a total absence of the kind of love which suggests mutual respect and emotional bonds of any lasting nature. Such aircraft art, as in fact all art, is of course no more than an extension of self, self-expression or wish-fulfillment. In the case of the pin-up it offers the male viewer an image of what many like himself hope for but will in fact seldom find in real life. That is the woman they can dominate, indeed is waiting to be dominated, who 'won't answer back, or demand reciprocation, compromise, or fair treatment,' [said] Mark Gabor [in his book] *The Pin Up: A Modest History*, 1973.

"In short the male's deepest and perhaps basest dreams, especially during periods of stress as found in combat, are of times and environments which offer security and clear mastery of the situation. . . . Being labeled as it has and having been given a very personal identity the aircraft now takes the place of the submissive dream girl. To face death or the threat of death regularly presents a kind of insecurity many find difficult, to say the least, to deal with emotionally. Going into combat then a crewman or crew must at least retain some 'faith' or emotional security in the impersonal machine, their aircraft, which they hope to control and use, uncompromisingly, to their own ends. By offering the aircraft the mythical identity of their 'dream girl' they are thereby insuring, superstitiously at least, a partial control or male dominance over the most critical part of a crew's environment—the aircraft itself."

Regardless of the psychological explanations for what makes nose art so important to morale or why it all happened, we offer a tour through this fascinating world without trying to find all the answers. It exists because it exists, a part of human experience that refuses to be buried, particularly in times of war.

Chapter 1

Why Nose Art?

A Psychologist's View

by George R. Klare

When Jeff Ethell asked if I would be interested in writing a chapter for this book on nose art, my quick response was yes. The question came during an aviation tour he led to England in the fall of 1989, with visits to a number of air bases and museums. Of special interest to me was going to see what remained of the 100th Bomb Group's air base in Thorpe Abbotts, since I flew from that base in World War II as a B–17 navigator. Most of what had been the base has now been returned to its former use, farming. The few remaining buildings, however, have been restored and made into a fine memorial to the famous old Bloody Hundredth by Britons who live nearby. My emotion almost overwhelmed me as I finally "signed in" from my last, unfinished mission on December 31, 1944. I was shot down on that date and parachuted into Germany, where I

During Operation Desert Storm, the long and influential shadow of Alberto Vargas fell across another generation of combat aircraft. Here, Vargas' June 1943 *Esquire* gatefold reclines in resurrected form as *Sweet Sixteen* on a 135th AREFG KC-135 on duty in the war zone from Knoxville, Tennessee. *USAF, T/Sgt. D. S. McMichael*

spent the rest of World War II as a prisoner of war.

During most of the forty-five years since, I felt little interest in going to see the base, or even other places connected with my wartime experiences. I was busy with a family and a career as a university dean and professor of psychology. I actually went back to England at least half a dozen times during that period, as a lecturer at the Open University's headquarters in Milton Keynes, as the holder of a Fulbright grant later for research there, and as a visitor in Europe. But I never returned to Thorpe Abbotts: getting there was too difficult, and I thought what I might find if I did get there would prove disappointing. When I took the tour in 1989, however, I had retired and had begun to reflect more on WW II. I even became, I guess, a 100th Bomb "groupie" as do so many aging veterans of their own wartime unit. So the return to Thorpe Abbotts was nostalgic, and in the flush of feeling I said yes, I would be pleased to write the chapter.

I would like to say that part of my desire came from the nose art on

the bomber in which I flew. In fact, however, my crew and I were shot down before we had a particular B–17 assigned to us, and our plane on that day had only the designation 231895 LD-Y. We were still considered a replacement crew, and thus still flew different airplanes on our missions. I was only vaguely aware of nose art then, as I recall, never having been directly involved with selecting or implementing any. Whatever my knowledge then, the long interval since erased most of the remainder of it. So my first serious question to myself later was "What do you know about nose art?" and my second question was "What perspective could you add to what has already been published?"

Addressing the first question, fortunately I now collect publications about the US Army Air Corps in general as well as the Eighth Air Force and the 100th Bomb Group in particular, giving me several hundred reproductions of nose art to peruse. Gary Valant's *Vintage Aircraft Nose Art* later also gave me a thousand or so examples to review. As for the second question, I was trained in psychology, and psychologists regularly stick their noses into various aspects of human behavior, so why not into nose art? My point of view will be that of a psychologist looking at the motivation for nose art, tempered by the experience of a WW II airman who flew in a B-17 in combat—for a while at least. One more comment: psychologists are sometimes characterized as persons likely to spin Freudian tales about why such-and-so kind of human activity occurred. These can be serious as well as titillating, as were Sigmund Freud's own suggestions of the unconscious association between flying and male sexuality in his lectures at the University of Vienna during the winter sessions of 1915-17 (*A General Introduction to Psycho-Analysis.* New York: Liveright, 1935, page 138).

I do not intend to take this approach to nose art, however. Readers who wish to see an authoritative, thorough-going Freudian account of combat flyers and flying generally in World War II can find one in Douglas Bond's *The Love and Fear of Flying* (New York: International Universities Press, 1952). I will try, in my analysis, to remain as objective as possible under the circumstances. That does not, I hope, mean my review of this inherently fascinating topic will be any the less interesting.

So why did fliers put paintings on their airplanes? Before I began my review I recalled only, and thus assumed, that nose art meant scantily dressed, busty females placed on the pilot's side of the nose of bombers. My memories were of mammaries, you might say. A psychological explanation would not be needed in such a case, I felt, except perhaps to add "Aha" or "Hmmm" or some such

response. My review, however, showed nose art to be much more complex. My easy assumptions about where paintings were placed, how they were chosen, and who made them all proved too simple. So, before getting into the question of why nose art, some background information based on my review and analysis of the examples available to me.

The first point is that many of the best-known examples of nose art do involve the human adult female, but as only one of many subjects. My review of well over a thousand examples showed about 55 percent were female figures, with about one-fourth of them nude and most of the rest partially clothed. Four-legged animals, birds, and insects (such as bees or hornets) made up almost 15 percent of the total. Another 30 percent or so involved such varied subjects as cartoon characters (for instance, Dogpatch), babies and children, death symbols (such as the skull and crossbones), zodiacal signs, and devils or gremlins, to name a few of the more common among the hundred or so categories I found. Robert Bredau analyzed 769 samples of nose art in his thesis, and although he used four somewhat different categories his figures are comparable. For example, he found over 57 percent involved female figures and more than 11 percent male figures. He also found that about 11 percent had animal figures, and 7 percent had neutral figures (those not clearly male, female, or animal). He also reported names as motifs in themselves in over 12 percent of his examples.

A second observation is that nose art was usually painted on the noses of airplanes, but not always. Occasionally paintings appeared on or near the tail, and sometimes on both nose and tail, with the same or (rarely)

different paintings on these two places or even the two sides of the nose. At times, the paintings from airplanes also appeared on the backs of A-2 flight jackets, crew work stations such as guns or gun turrets, engine nacelles, or even the sides and ceilings of buildings at air bases.

Third, I found that the paintings on the nose did typically appear on the pilot's side, but not in all cases. Several sources say that the pilot usually picked, or at least had the final say on, the painting after discussion with his crew. The subject sometimes reflected a noteworthy characteristic of the pilot as well, but some choices were based on one or another crew member's idiosyncracies or honored someone else entirely. Many subjects, however, did not depend upon such personal considerations, occasionally reflecting instead the local environment (for instance, a Panamanian archway in a squadron assigned to the Canal Zone, or the Asian look of the females in South Pacific nose art). In some cases the ground crew actually made the choices when the air crew was tardy in making them.

Fourth, a specific painting generally appeared on only one airplane, but with exceptions. Some of the paintings were duplicated intentionally, often with such designations as I and II, but for somewhat contradictory reasons. The nose art on an aircraft that had successfully carried a fortunate crew through the required number of missions was seldom changed, for example, and was even likely to be duplicated on other aircraft. On the other hand, combat misfortune might have claimed the first airplane carrying a particular painting, or at least made it unsuitable for further missions, opening the way for a second use of the painting. Duplications also arose, however, because an available painter (most often a crew member at one or another base) was skilled in painting that particular subject and not others. And, of course, certain genre such as Varga or Petty girls, or particular pin-up subjects, such as Betty Grable, became popular and artists who could do skillful reproductions were much sought after.

A fifth factor is that paintings typically bore names or nicknames, often that of the pilot's or other crew member's girlfriend (such as the famous *Memphis Belle*). The paintings that appeared alone often seemed intended as an integral part of an airplane's appearance or reputation. An example is the tiger-shark mouth painted on the P–40s of the Flying Tigers, the American Volunteer Group before WW II, and the subsequent Fourteenth Air Force of WW II. When used, names corresponded with the paintings in almost, but not quite all cases (I do not know how to explain this lack of agreement). Paul Andrews has carefully tracked down as many of the names as he could find given to B–17 or B–24 aircraft assigned to the Eighth Air Force, finally listing some 2,600. Of special significance for analytical purposes, names appeared alone in at least 25 percent of the examples of nose art I reviewed, but certainly many more, since aircraft with names alone were much less likely to be memorialized in publications. President George Bush's wartime TBM Avenger, incidentally, provided one of the picture-less examples; it carried only the name Barbara.

A final point is that all combat airplanes, whether or not they had paintings, names, or nicknames, had number designations. Where bombers were concerned, at least, they carried only these numbers, with occasional added letters, unless nose art and/or names were added at some stage. Many aircraft—exactly how many is not clear—never had nose art. My review of the airplanes assigned to the 100th Bomb Group showed that only about half (55 percent) ever had nose art. Perhaps that corroborated the accuracy of the Bloody Hundredth's reputation, but my review indicates these proportions held for most groups in the Eighth Air Force. I have the impression that the planes delivered earlier to the 100th were more likely to have ended up with names than those delivered later, which may also have been rather common. Perhaps the novelty may have worn off somewhat, or perhaps those of us who flew mostly during an English winter were less likely to try to paint nose art. The short days, the damp cold, the sticky mud, and the occasional snow made such outdoor activity less likely than in the summer. The rationing of coal made it hard enough to be comfortable inside our hut!

What are we to make of this jumble of partly expected and partly unexpected observations? First, all manner of special circumstances existed. Second, they suggest that a look at some historical background might be helpful before drawing conclusions about the motivation for nose art.

To begin, strong parallels exist between the earlier ships that traveled the seas and the later ships that traveled the air. Thus it seems natural for terminology and practices from the former to carry over to the latter. One of the more amusing of these was the christening, in the manner of ocean-going ships, of at least several aircraft during WW II. Both Jimmy Cagney and Edward G. Robinson christened B–17s bearing their names. Recalling the fragility of the plexiglass and the thin skin of the nose reminds me that they must have had to choose carefully the spot to christen.

More significantly, most ships that travel the sea even now carry names or titles, and many at one time also bore what came to be called "figurehead" carvings on the prow. Furthermore, the fact that sea ships have long been referred to in female terms such as "she" or "her" doubtless made it natural to refer to air ships that way also. Freud has already suggested why "vessels" might carry such female terminology, so we can turn to the next question: Could the practice of naming airplanes and painting nose art on them be a simple carryover from ships that travel the sea? Possibly. The common observation that many of the sea art figureheads consisted of busty and lightly clad females seems to prefigure the painting of undraped or lightly clad females on the noses of aircraft. What does that tell us?

Sexual deprivation, or at least diversion, clearly played a major role in nose art as in earlier sea art, true. But did sex as such provide the underlying reason for nose art? The picture does not seem all that clear. As noted, female figures appeared in only a little over half the examples available in Bredau's and my independent analyses. Also, at least some of the females celebrated were mothers (*Enola Gay*, for example) and babies or very young girls. Furthermore, some of the paintings of adult females did not have an overtly sexual emphasis, or at least not an obvious one. For example, there were well-known or well-liked personages, typically fully dressed, and even an occasional "warrior woman."

My own view is that the psychological mechanism of identification was a more inclusive reason for nose art. Crew members on the sea or in the air wanted to see their complex ships as almost human entities with which they could identify. Especially when they faced danger, they even wanted to endow their ships with almost superhuman qualities to protect them and bring them safely back. Certainly many references made by combat crewmen to the B-17 (with which I am most familiar) carried that kind of connotation. The nicknames "Flying Fortress" and "Queen of the Skies" were the most common. Recall too that Charles Lindbergh's story of his solo crossing of the Atlantic was titled *We*. This need to identify with a ship also appeared among ground crew, who felt a strong sense of responsibility for the safe performance of their airplane and sweated out missions along with the air crew.

Equally if not more important, nose art and names made it possible for airmen to identify somewhat more readily with each other and feel pride and confidence as a crew. Developing strong relationships among crew members was always a goal in air crew training. In fact, when a particular crew member did not get along well with, or have the confidence of, the rest of the crew a transfer often resulted. Members of a combat crew needed to depend upon each other, and identification with their airplane helped to create strong interdependence among crew members. The crew itself also replaced home security influences in some cases, and afforded a bulwark against homesickness. Some members of these young crews found themselves away from home for the first extended stay in their lives, and

14

for the first time faced death directly and personally.

Superstitious behavior consequently became another aspect of identification. Just as professional athletes do, air crew members often had rituals meant to bring good luck or, more important in combat, ward off bad luck. For example, a member of my crew regularly put his chewing gum alongside the rear door of our B-17 just before we began a mission. After we were shot down, he lamented not having done so that day.

The choice of fierce or protective names or paintings seems to be part of this sort of ritual, as can be seen in the kinds of four-legged animals and even six-legged insects chosen. Occasionally one of these designations either had, or grew to have, an unlucky connotation, and air crew members were known to shun such an airplane and dread having to fly in it. Logic dictated that chance played a major part in a bomber crew's survival in combat, but emotion often made such lack of control unacceptable. Superstitious behavior involving a favorite airplane seemed to mean good luck, at least until a fatalistic attitude developed.

Naming or painting an airplane illustrates another aspect of identification, ease of reference. Crew members found a memorable name easier to identify with, and thus refer to, than a mere number. Along this line, note that the Wright brothers gave the first successful airplane a name, *The Flyer*. Others followed suit. Glenn Curtiss flew the *June Bug*, Wiley Post the *Winnie Mae*, and Charles Lindbergh the *Spirit of St. Louis*. The more recent space shuttles also carry their own names, making them much easier to identify and talk about.

But if identification could be achieved by naming alone, why go to the trouble of painting art on the nose of airplanes? What could painting add?

Some kinds of painting could, of course, add another dimension of identification—identification as part of a friendly squadron. During WW I the members of the famous "Hat in the Ring" squadron doubtless wanted to be more easily identified by their logo as superior pilots. During WW II, the increased speed of combat clashes made such identification more difficult, which is why so much time was spent in training gunners on bombers to recognize fighters at a distance by their silhouettes alone. Otherwise, enemy fighters could slip in close enough to inflict damage to a bomber before being clearly recognized by their markings, and then it might be too late for defensive action. Worse yet, gunners might too easily mistake friendly fighters as enemies and attempt, in the stress of combat, to shoot them down. Most often, therefore, the group markings on such places as the tails of bombers served primarily a friendly purpose. They provided a vital aid in the building of formations for missions and in helping bombers stay close together in these formations when weather or stress made this difficult.

Mention must be made of fighter pilots who used painting, instead, to make their identity as enemies more quickly and clearly known. The paintings on the noses of the Flying Tiger fighters in WW II have already been mentioned. In World War I the German pilots of the famous Flying Circuses applied bright red paint to help identify their aircraft. The German pilots of World War II, whom we called the Abbeville Boys, followed the same pattern. They painted the entire noses of their German fighters bright yellow so they could more easily be identified by enemy bomber crews. These pilots wanted to, and did, strike fear into air crews who knew of their prowess in shooting down bombers.

One might be tempted to think that painting on bombers would be counterproductive in the sense that enemy fliers might more easily single out a particular airplane, or especially a group, for an attack. This hypothesis has been raised in the case of the Bloody Hundredth Group, with its distinctive D in a square on the tail. Could this marking have made the Hundredth a marked group? Why else would it have suffered such infamous massacres? Other evidence, however, including that from surviving German air crew members, suggests that combat attacks occurred too rapidly and indiscriminately in most cases for such identifying marks to make much of a difference. This was apparently true even in the supposed case of singling out the 100th, where the entire Group of B–17s was marked in the same way. Nose art could hardly add undesirable identification, therefore. Possible exceptions might be the early use of a few nicknames such as "Murder, Inc." German propagandists found them a valuable aid in characterizing airmen as *terrorfliegers*, causing nicknames of this sort to be banned.

Painting of entire airplanes early in WW II involved what might be thought of as a negative rather than positive aspect of identification—camouflage. The tops of bombers, for example, carried irregular, colored patterns so a fighter pilot above could not so easily distinguish them from the ground below. The bottoms, on the other hand, carried different colored patterns so that they could more readily fade into the sky above. Later in WW II such painting was abandoned because the size of bomber formations made them hard to hide from enemy fighter pilots or radar operators, anyway. The paint simply added too much useless weight. Ground installations could be usefully camouflaged, but not bombers.

If the painting on bombers did not provide this kind of desirable or undesirable identification to the enemy, what could nose art add to what names or titles already provided? Well, for one obvious thing, a picture could be worth a thousand words, at least to airmen viewing a painting of a desirable female. Nose art also served as decoration, and follow-the-leader status needs of young airmen played a part in the growth of this practice. Why else would crews have been so careful to get a skilled artist when possible? Or even go so far as to let a skilled artist choose the subject of the painting as one that would fit his or her particular skill or preference?

Nose art can be traced back to at least World War I, though some argue that the paintings then were basically squadron insignia. Nose art of the World War II sort, at least, could not be found on the bombers and fighters of the US Army Air Corps prior to that time. Why, then, the more "risque business" of nose art in WW II, to use Phil Cohan's term? Changes in feelings and attitudes during wartime clearly played a role. Moral controls weakened, for several reasons. Death and disablement became more prominent and probable, and a fling thus more acceptable. Soldiers often found themselves away from home, and their behavior could not be as easily observed as before. Besides, those still at home could not so readily criticize those out fighting for them. As a consequence, winking at activities and behavior previously unacceptable became more common. So, when air crew members painted naked or nearly naked females on their airplanes, who could say no? Weren't they risking their lives for just this kind of freedom? Wasn't this, to use the phrase of the day, one of the things they were fighting for?

But society did then, and does today, set some limits in condoning such behavior. Wilfrid Sheed put it well in referring to entertainers' comments during World War II (*Essays in Disguise*, New York: Alfred A. Knopf, 1990): "Girls had curves, oh Lord, they had curves (Bob Hope must have kept a warehouse full of curve jokes) but no cracks or fissures." Nose art breached that limit on a few airplanes, but cautiously, as Melissa Keiser reported in an interview for a newspaper article (*The Washington Times*, January 20, 1989). Nose art got more daring with greater distance from high headquarters, she noted, comparing USAAF aircraft in England with those way out in the South Pacific. Also, she reported, a particular combat bomber's nose art would occasionally need to have certain strategic items of apparel added when the airplane returned stateside for a war bond promotional tour. Some crews angrily painted "Censored" over their airplane's nose art rather than add clothing.

What has happened to nose art since World War II? As this rationale involving society-imposed limits at given times in history would suggest, it all but disappeared except during the wartime periods of the Korean and Vietnam conflicts. At least until 1985, when a Strategic Air Command regulation permitted it again as a morale-builder. But not, as this rationale would again suggest, in the free-spirited mode of WW II. The regulation says that nose art must be in good taste, and apparently most of the recent examples have been. Commanders strongly encouraged the use of historical names, nicknames, and subjects for the paintings.

Some recent examples, however, appear to be at least suggestive if not downright improper by today's standards. True to form, these have been justified by their distance from the controlling effect of high headquarters, either physically (for instance, in the cold Upper Peninsula of Michigan) or militarily (in Air National Guard units). And complaints have been voiced. One National Women's History Project representative was quoted as saying

she had hoped that chapter [World War II nose art] had been closed (*The Washington Times*, January 20, 1989). And one can imagine the objections likely to be raised in Saudi Arabia if suggestive nose art became publicized on US aircraft there. Or ships. Why the equivalent of nose art appeared infrequently on the vessels of World War II (except possibly Army tankers), and is still not found on US Navy ships, raises some interesting speculations.

As might have been expected in the case of nose art, however, the other side of today's sexual mores has surfaced. Two Air Force women have been quoted as saying they could be mollified if just one airplane had a

likeness of a well-muscled, half-nude man (*Air Force Times*, February 27, 1989). Such a painting is apparently on the way, which is not surprising since one of the two women is the pilot of a tanker and the other an artist who paints nose art.

With the recent re-introduction of nose art and the greater freedom of sexual expression today, who knows how far wartime nose art might go? Identification in its several forms, and females in their own desirable forms, can account for much of the answer to the question "Why nose art?" in World War II. Adding war in helps to complete the picture, but emphasizing it takes much of the pleasure out. So for now, enough analysis; why not just enjoy the nose art in this book?

Chapter 2

World War I to 1940

The Beginnings

Italy was the first country to use aircraft in war when several were deployed to Tripoli in 1912, and by 1913 a number of squadrons were using unit and identification markings. A Nieuport-Macchi of the Italian Navy, serial number M13041, was painted like a sea monster with a face, teeth, eyes, and large ears, behind which the number 20 was painted in large black numerals. In addition, the Italians marked the aircraft with 1x5 in. white wound stripes for each bullet hole received in combat. Nothing has ever been quite the same since.

When World War I began in 1914 aircraft markings were barely considered necessary. Just two years earlier the French initiated a system of tricolored roundels to be painted on their aircraft as national markings. It wasn't until after the shooting started and the machines of all sides were being hit by both enemy and friendly fire that the other nations followed suit, as much out of self-protection as anything else.

In August 1914 the Royal Flying Corps (RFC) joined the British Expeditionary Force in France but other than the addition of factory serial numbers, little else was applied to the aircraft doped fabric as pilots of opposing sides passed each other, trying to take pot shots as best they could. The very first RFC markings were the Union Jack, at first painted on at the pilot's discretion in various sizes and locations.

With the introduction of the synchronized machine gun and true fighter aircraft, things changed rapidly. Since deadly German Fokker E-type monoplanes were similar in appearance to French Morane Type N machines, by early 1916 French and British squadrons started painting the

Contrary to common memory, nose art was sometimes very flamboyant during World War I, though not on the majority of aircraft. Here American Capt. Harry S. Gwinne, commanding officer of Aviation Field No. 4, 3rd Aerial Instruction Center, stands next to his Nieuport 24bis *The Flying Fish* at Issoudun, France, on May 21, 1918. *Signal Corps via Peter M. Bowers*

cowlings, cabane struts, undercarriage legs, and wheel covers a bright red as an ID marking. Later in the year all sides were introducing camouflage paint and unit markings.

French motor transport units were the first to use a form of stylized identification, painted on the sides of their vans. A young, idealistic volunteer ambulance driver and fledgling artist named Walt Disney painted his own vehicle's canvas sides with personal art. These unit insignia, particularly those on the sides of ambulances, were so well done in depicting nurses, Indian heads, cartoon characters, and animals that French aircraft squadrons quickly applied similar, if not identical, motifs.

Though the Royal Flying Corps was the first to introduce numbers and letters on the sides of their aircraft, for the rest of the war the British rarely applied anything more colorful. On the other hand, the Belgians, French, Italians, and Russians used unit symbols as a departure to embellish their mounts with a colorful variety of emblems. Early in the war, individualistic pieces of art began to appear which were unique to the pilot.

Back in the United States, veterans decorated their personal aircraft during the war. This Curtiss JN-4H flown by instructor Major Boots carried art directly related to his name—*Boots To The Kaiser. Signal Corps via Peter M. Bowers*

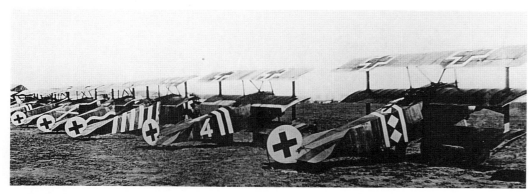

Nothing else in the First World War equaled the German Flying Circus series of individual markings. Following the lead of the legendary Manfred von Richthofen, German fighter pilots applied the colors of the rainbow to their aircraft, almost daring Allied pilots to pick them out individually. This line of Jasta 19 Fokker Dr.I triplanes in late March or early April 1918 shows fuselage crosses deleted to make room for personal markings, while each aircraft carries unit yellow and black bands and white cowlings. The triplane at the far right was flown by Ltn.d.R. Arthur Rahn, and the third with white candy striping may have been Leutnant Rienau's fighter. *Peter M. Bowers*

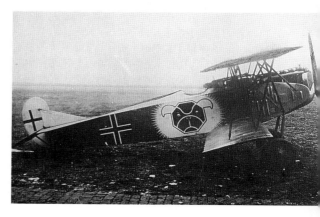

Faces were a favorite, as this stylized dog on a Fokker D.VII shows. *Nowarra via Peter M. Bowers*

In spite of their general lack of color, the British were the first to name individual aircraft. No. 10 (naval) Squadron's Black Flight of black overall painted Sopwith Triplanes became famous when its core of five Canadians painted names on the side. *Black Maria* was flown by Raymond Collishaw, *Black Death* by J. E. Sharman, *Black Sheep* by J. E. Nash, *Black Roger* by Ellis Reid, and *Black Prince* by M. Alexander. Collishaw finished the war with sixty kills as the Empire's second leading surviving ace behind fellow Canadian Billy Bishop who had seventy-two kills.

The real surprise of the war, however, took place in late 1916 and early 1917 when Allied pilots started to return from missions with reports of encountering brightly colored, outlandish, even fantastic German fighters painted every color of the rainbow. The German *Jagdstaffeln* (fighter units), on an incredible victory streak which peaked during what the RFC remembered as Bloody April 1917, were allowing their pilots to paint their fighters in any combination of colors they could dream up.

The trend was initiated by Oswald Boelcke, who painted his Halberstadt blue, then imitated by Manfred von Richthofen with his red Albatros D.III. Before long the baron's Jasta 11 pilots were using some form of red on their aircraft, with the understanding that only his aircraft remained red overall. Soon other *Jagdstaffeln* were following with not only what became known as the Flying Circus rainbow of colors but also individual pieces of art painted on the aircraft at the pilots' request.

There was little worry about negating the effects of the normal camouflage which was, at times, completely covered. Second Lt. D. G.

Lewis, a Sopwith Camel pilot with No. 3 Squadron, RAF, who became von Richthofen's eightieth and final kill on April 20, 1918, survived to recall the encounter in Dale M.

Titler's book, *The Day the Red Baron Died* (1970): "As soon as we had shot past the enemy formation and turned to select an opponent, I knew we had met Richthofen's famed Circus. The

Werner Voss (right) stands next to his famous Fokker triplane in September 1917 when Jasta 10 was transitioning from the older Pfalz D.III behind him. His Dr.I was unique in having a stylized face painted on the cowling, which took advantage of the two large upper cooling holes. *Aerofax via Jay Miller*

The large bombers that emerged during the war were excellent airframes upon which to begin the airman's tradition of nose art, with noses unencumbered by engines. This German Friedrichs-Hafen G.II, in the 1917–18 time period, has an entire face painted on the nose. *Peter M. Bowers*

The Fokker D.VII of Gefreiter Scheutzel, Jasta 65, was far ahead of its time in carrying well-defined art on both sides of the fuselage. The characters depict the Grimms fairy tale, "The Seven Swabians," while the crest on top of the fuselage may be a version of the Wurttemberg Coat of Arms (light yellow antlers on a black crest?). The fuselage is overpainted, perhaps in gray, while the nose and tail may be chocolate brown. *Via Greg VanWyngarden*

Lt. Georg von Hantelmann's Albatros D.V of Jasta 15 (or possibly 18) was very colorful indeed—Prussian blue fuselage with a red nose (unit colors)—with a skull to indicate his former service in the "Death's Head Hussars," Regt. No. 17. *H. H. Wynne via Greg VanWyngarden*

planes were painted all colors of the rainbow, each to personally identify the pilot. One was painted like a draughtboard with black and white squares. Another was all sky blue. One looked like a dragon's head and large eyes were painted on the engine cowling. Others had lines in various colors running along the fuselages or across them; machines painted black and red, dark blue, gray. There was a yellow nosed one too. Richthofen, of course, led the formation in his Fokker triplane painted a brilliant pillar-box red. Its black crosses were edged with white."

Soon Belgian, French, Russian, and Polish Nieuports, then Spads, were sporting their pilots' heraldry, living up to a grand medieval tradition as Knights of the Air. The variety and originality was overpowering, much of it foreshadowing another war to come

with a number of nude female and cartoon character motifs.

By the time the United States entered the war in the air during its last year, American squadrons followed suit, though less flamboyantly, in the tradition of the famous Lafayette Escadrille. A series of unit emblems were created in the field reflecting the frontier spirit of the young nation—Indian heads, bucking broncos, kicking mules, massive bisons, Uncle Sam's hat-in-the-ring. In looking back at the war Ralph Linton, in his article titled "Totemism and the A.E.F.," *American Anthropologist*, 1921, saw the development of US Army unit insignia paralleling that of North American Indian tribal totem poles and carvings with very similar motifs. These unit emblems were quickly painted on the sides of the aircraft in colorful, enlarged fashion

so that there was no mistaking which squadron was in the air.

Typical of American airmen, they painted these insignia on their aircraft without official authorization. It was not until a year after the Armistice in November 1919 that the Army got around to approving the first fifty-five squadron insignia.

With rare exception, from the end of World War I to the beginning of World War II, personal markings disappeared. Unit insignia remained, often just as striking as what would later become known as nose art but still well within official boundaries.

The Spanish Civil War, lasting from 1936 to 1939, reawakened the combat pilot's need to name and decorate his machine. Luftwaffe crews, flying for the Nationalists or rebels under Gen. Francisco Franco, painted a number of individual motifs,

Sister Erna visits her brother, Lt. Hans-Joachim von Hippel with his Albatros D.V at Jasta 5, Boistrancourt airfield. The aircraft's silver-gray fuselage carried a red dragon with unit markings of a green tail with red border and red spinner. Wings were green and mauve with pale blue undersides and white chevron on the top wing. *Norm S. Burtt via Greg VanWyngarden*

The Albatros D.Va of Lt. Otto Fuchs, CO of Jasta 77b, carried a light blue tail unit marking with his personal fox insignia (Fuchs translates to fox) chasing the

Gallic cock. The rest of the fuselage was doped plywood while the wings were green and mauve. *Via Greg VanWyngarden*

particularly those drawn from popular cartoon and comic strip characters. Adolf Galland's unit, 3/J88, had Mickey Mouse painted on its Heinkel 51s. The mouse, chomping on a cigar and carrying a battle axe in one hand and a pistol in the other, later became

Shark mouths appeared on military aircraft almost as soon as the first shots were fired in anger. This AEG.IV, 1917–18, was particularly well suited for nose art with a broad, unobstructed nose. *Via Don Malko*

A rare, sharp view of one of World War I's most famous pieces of personal art, the morbid representation of death carried on the side of French ace Charles Nungesser's Nieuport fighters. *Aerofax via Jay Miller*

Virginia was an S.E.5a assigned to the American 25th Aero Squadron at the end of the war.

Just after the end of World War I, American fighter squadrons experienced their own brief Flying Circus period by painting incredibly garish individual schemes on their aircraft. This line of 94th Aero Squadron Spad XIIIs in occupied Germany, March 1919, speaks for itself. *Peter M. Bowers*

Lieutenant Jeffers stands next to his 94th Aero Squadron Spad XIII which carried red, white, and blue bursts emanating

from the national roundels. *Jeffers via Sloan and Bowers*

Though no doubt it irked freedom-loving Walt Disney, his cartoon characters crossed all national boundaries and Mickey Mouse showed up on both sides of the Spanish Civil War, something that would happen again a short time later during World War II. This Spanish Republican Air Force Polikarpov I-15 carries a particularly faithful 1930s rendition of the famous rodent. *NASM*

Galland's personal marking.

Mickey appeared just as happily on the loyalist or Republican side. A Polikarpov I-15 serial number CA-142, based at Barajas Aerodrome, near Madrid, Spain, had the famous mouse painted on its tail with a light bulb just above his nose. The International Brigade Squadron, with several American pilots, featured Popeye in a boxing stance on the tail of Polikarpov I-16 serial number CM-274.

However, not until the invasion of Poland, then the attack on Pearl Harbor, did airmen find the ultimate endless stretch of metal canvases upon which to express their feelings.

During the late 1930s the US Army Air Corps continued a tradition of carrying only squadron heraldry on its aircraft. On the whole these insignia were very colorful, particularly against a bare

aluminum fuselage, as can be seen with this Selfridge Field, Michigan, based 94th Pursuit Squadron, 1st Group Curtiss P-36A Hawk, June 22, 1939. *Harland Wood via Norm Taylor*

23

Chapter 3

World War II

The Golden Age

After listening to some of the aircrews who fought in World War II, one might conclude the war couldn't have been won without the pin-up and the aircraft nose art it inspired. Though, as George Klare pointed out in chapter 1, there were almost as many examples of nose art without them, girls served as the prime movers for this phenomenon of flying personalized aircraft into combat.

Pin-ups came from numerous sources, but most likely George Petty's art in *Esquire* magazine through 1941 spawned the avalanche that followed. By the end of 1941 Alberto Vargas had supplanted Petty, and *Esquire* launched the Varga Girl straight into a world war through its pages, including special military editions of the magazine and calendars. Other artists, particularly

Joltin' Josie The Pacific Pioneer was the 498th BG B–29 that brought airpower planner Gen. Haywood Hansell to Saipan. On April 1, 1945, while being flown by Capt. Wilson Currier's crew, a small explosion was seen shortly after takeoff and the bomber burst into flames, crashing into Magicienne Bay. *Edward T. Donnelly via Steve Birdsall*

the talented Gillette A. "Gil" Elvgren, contributed heavily to the stream of calendars and pin-ups. *Yank*, the GI's own news magazine, ran full-page photo pinups in every issue. That single page was so popular it wallpapered huts and was tacked to tent poles around the globe.

When Glenn Miller was touring the war zones with his Army Air Forces band in 1944, the pin-up was so much a part of the American war effort that he added "Peggy the Pin-Up Girl" to his repertoire: "Oh, this sweet little chick is the pick of the crew, And she just suits the taste of the waist gunner too. They were there in the air over Berlin, and the voice sounded clear as a pearl: 'Pilot to bombardier, come on boys, let's drop one here, For Peggy, the Pin-Up Girl!' "

Throughout the war as American aviation units entered the combat zones, the noses of their aircraft carried expanded versions of the "ideal" well-proportioned woman as well as cartoon characters, animals, patriotic slogans, and a host of subjects which seemed to lack nothing in variety. At first, names and art were

governed by general common sense but as the war progressed, particularly in the isolated regions of the Pacific, the lack of peacetime restraint resulted in ever more suggestive art. This resulted in AAF Regulation 35–22, August 1944, which stated:

2. *Policy.* The custom of decorating organizational equipment of the Army Air Force with individual characteristic design is authorized by the Secretary of War (memorandum from the Adjutant General, dated 19 December 1942) and is encouraged as a means of increasing morale.

3. *Definitions*:
   a. "Equipment" as used herein means operating equipment, i.e. airplanes.
   b. "Design" or "Organizational Design" as used herein refers to the markings applied to organizational equipment and does not refer to group or other unit coats of arms not to uniform insignia or shoulder or sleeve insignia covered by AR 600–40.

This sounded very official and made the Army brass happy but there

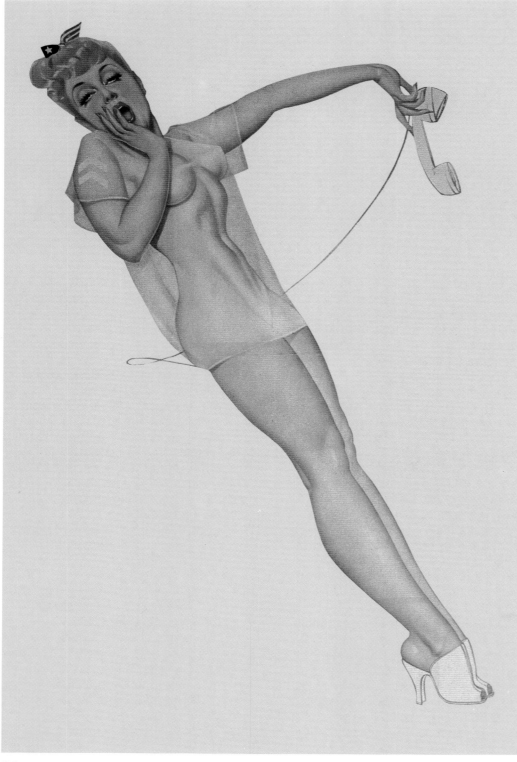

was virtually no effect on how nose art was applied in the field.

Though Navy and Marine aircraft did have some nose art applied, this was far more the exception than the rule. When the original USN directive on camouflage and markings came out long before World War II, the regulations were very specific that no markings other than squadron badges and national insignia would be applied—this meant *none*. That regulation still holds to the present day but the rules have been broken at various times while, for the most part, those in command have looked the other way. This was particularly true of the long-range land-based Ventura and Privateer patrol squadrons in the Pacific where crews seldom saw the brass.

When Charles A. Lindbergh arrived in New Guinea during the summer of 1944 as a civilian advisor, he was aghast. As he recalled in his journal for June 20, he drove down Topline airstrip "through the long lines of planes parked in revetments. The cheapness of the emblems and names painted on the bombers and fighters nauseates me at times— mostly naked women or 'Donald Ducks'—names such as 'Fertile Myrtle' under a large and badly painted figure of a reclining nude." When photos of these aircraft leaked out stateside, there was some measure of attempted official displeasure, particularly when civilians complained, but overall not much changed until the war was over.

Esquire magazine launched World War II nose art as it came to be defined by sheer numbers. Its gatefolds and calendars by George Petty, who worked as the magazine's primary artist before Pearl Harbor, set the standards with his Petty Girl, as exhibited here by his gatefold wizardry. *Copyright Esquire Associates*

In the service papers published by GIs for GIs, the attitude toward this rapidly growing American phenomenon bordered on delight. In the August 5, 1943 issue of *The Stars and Stripes*, Andrew A. Rooney (yes, same Andy Rooney of CBS News' "60 Minutes") wrote an article entitled "Nudes, Names and Numbers" with his usual flair: "Grim-faced Luftwaffe pilots proud of the guts that take them within the suicide circle of a Fortress formation, determined to do or die for the Fatherland, must wonder what the hell kind of an Air Force they are up against. They come driving in, teeth clenched, hell bent for Hitler, and along with a hail of lead they are greeted by the stupid grin of some absurd comic book character, or the nude form of a Petty girl painted on the nose of the bomber they are attacking. . . .

"[This nose art] could only originate in the minds of the men of one air force. The Forts aren't named for any particular reason and no one in particular names them. It is a very American process.

"A pilot from Maine is apt to come out any rainy morning and find that his plane has been named *Texas*. Or the quiet teetotaler who quit divinity school to join the Air Force is

This page and following page
In 1940 *Esquire* introduced a new artist to its pages and by the time the war started, Alberto Vargas had become the magazine's sole master of the female form, as seen in these calendar pages from August 1941 and October 1943. The Varga Girl (*Esquire* dropped the "s" and made a trademark out of the artist's name) became the most duplicated subject for aircraft nose art through the millions of copies that made their way through the squadrons until the end of the war.
Copyright Esquire Associates via Charles Martignette

apt to come out on the line and find a nude stretching from the plastic nose to the pilot's compartment because his tail gunner (who did not quit divinity school to join the Air Force) knew a guy in Site Six who used to be a commercial artist in St. Louis and could still draw a plenty sexy nude."

This freestyle artistic expression got people in trouble, much to the disgust of serving combat and line crews. As Rooney reported, *Mr.*

Cesspool was the cause of a fight. Cesspool was a character straight out of *Li'l Abner* back when Daisy Mae was behind the eight ball in the hands of Carimee Back, from Old Virginny. One day some brass was making a tour of the field, and *Mr. Cesspool* was parked in a prominent place on the runway. The suggestion was made that the names on the planes should be ones that could be used in conversations—as tea in Claridge's.

"Some colonel or lieutenant colonel picked up the suggestion and went overboard with it. For a few brief hours there were to be no more names on planes that couldn't be bantered about in mixed company. No more *Vulgar Virgins* or *T.S.*'s. It would take a shipment of paint to cover the Fort names you wouldn't kick around in your living room, but fortunately the order fell flat and the names stand. If the brass had been up on their *Li'l Abner*, as they should have been, the whole episode might not have occurred."

By the end of World War II nose art had reached legendary status around the world, enjoyed by millions.

Upper left
Living nose art . . . so popular was the idea that most of the aircraft companies set up publicity shots like this one taken by Curtiss with a factory new SB2C Helldiver. *NASM*/Arnold

Before the United States got into World War II, Claire Chennault's American Volunteer Group, better known as the Flying Tigers, were preparing for battle over China with their former RAF Lend Lease Curtiss Tomahawks. With Walt Disney-designed winged tigers on the fuselage, shark mouths and squadron insignia in front of the cockpit, they flew into combat with the most colorful aircraft of the early war period. Here, three "Hell's Angels" Squadron Hawks cruise over China. *R. T. Smith*

What's In a Name

by Capt. Stanley Washburn,
Stars and Stripes, 1944

The finest writing to come out of the war thus far, according to *Of Mice and Men* Steinbeck, special writer for the *New York Herald Tribune*, is the illustrated literature appearing on the fuselages of the Boeing Fortress, Consolidated Liberator, North American Mitchell and Martin Marauder bombers of the Army Air Forces abroad. The thinking behind these names and illustrations is inspiring to read because it represents the very essence and spirit of the young, hell-bent-for-election American crews who fly and fight these ships and endow them with their own personalities.

The names, anecdotes and art work appearing on these war planes are so American that soldiers in the far east, in Africa and in England get homesick all over again just looking at them. The names bring back home memories of the familiar comic strip characters syndicated in home town newspapers from coast to coast—Corky, Superman, Popeye and the ever popular animals of the cartoon shorts shown in US movie houses—the Disney characters and that long-eared, carrot-chewing rabbit with the Bronx accent who is a very popular figure on the noses of our combat airplanes. The wise-cracking inscriptions and names also bring back memories of the Hit Parade tunes, the double talk of high school days and their girls—*Vibrant Virgin, Pistol Packin' Mama, Paper Doll* and just plain *Mary, Helen* and *Joho*.

In the past, the naming of ships has generally been a more or less sacred rite. Famous US warships were christened and names bearing a dignity appropriate to the history they later made. Such hallowed names as the *Constitution*, the *Bon Homme Richard*, the *Constellation* are a far cry from 1944's history making warships of the air, *Son of Satan, Myrtle the Fertile Turtle, Wham Wham Thank You Mam* and *Jabbo Skyking*.

The great majority of the bow decorations seen on the Liberator and Fortress bombers today still carry the female theme, but nowadays little or nothing is left to the imagination. The girls are all-American from their blond wavy curls to tinted toenails. They generally lie in languorous postures with arms under their heads and long, fascinating legs extending horizontally toward the pitot masts—reclining in sun-bathing position and costume. These fine girls are all unusually well developed specimens—a combination of the best features of the Varga and Petty girls, only with less clothing and executed on a scale large enough to make an infantry soldier's mouth water when the ship passes overhead even a thousand feet above.

Most Fortresses and Liberators to date are being ferried to the war zones by specialized trans-Atlantic crews of the Air Transport Command of the Army Air Forces and therefore arrive at their operating bases with no personality painted on them. Within a few days, however, this situation is corrected, although the art applied in the field is not as finished as it might be. Most of the Liberators, however, are being flown to the war from the US by the same tactical crews who will later fight the Japs and Nazis with them.

During the shake-down training over the southern fields throughout the US, these crews decide on a name and decorative theme and pay anywhere from $150 to $200 for skilled professional artists to air-brush or paint their dream girls on the spacious noses of their ships. The wise cracks under the combat positions for each crew member are added as history is made. For example, the name of the turret gunner on one Fortress as inscribed under his guns is "Pittman." After several raids over Germany the inscription is logically expanded to read "Pittman's Pew." The tail gunner of another Fort has "Helen and Bill" painted under the armored cubbyhole in the tail position. Before the war this same boy undoubtedly sported a roadster with "Helen" and "Bill" painted on the rear fenders. This fellow further adorned the tail section with that inscription often seen on the back of those Ford and Chevvy (sic) roadsters that used to pass you doing sixty in prewar days, "If you can read this, you're too damn close!"

When the rhetoric or art work is too pointed, it is censored by striking out the offending word or phrase with the stroke of a wide, red paint brush. The thus offended invariably prints "censored by . . ." beneath the deletion and notes the name of the officer guilty of the order to censor their ship.

One bomber, *Lulu*, appeared in Natal [Brazil] with one of the most intriguing female figures ever to grace canvas, paper or boudoir—only more so. This girl was provocatively poised, all rosy pink, in detail, and scaled up to about three times life size. Word spread through the camp. From the mess hall, from the tents and barracks, from the engine overhaul shelters, enlisted men, civilians, Brazilian workers, and officers streamed to the parked bomber to admire the epitome of American womanhood depicted on the nose section of this Liberator. That evening the commanding officer ordered the crew to make their girl more modest. "It wouldn't look right to the English to have that show up over there . . ." he explained. "Just paint some kind of a little something or other around her—well, fix it up some way before you take off. That's an order."

With singularly light hearts *Lulu*'s crew watched the artist among them, the top turret gunner, paint a neat, tight-fitting bathing suit on the girl. Two days later the same Liberator showed up in Africa, the girl completely unadorned in her naked splendor again, the object of every soldier's frustrated longing who came within vision of this Venus. Upon being asked what happened to the bathing suit that was painted on the girl at Natal, a crew member explained, "Oh, that was only water paint—we carry it with us for censoring purposes. When we went through that heavy rain in the equatorial front off the coast on the way over, it washed right off. *Lulu*'s a honey, ain't she?"

When *The Stars and Stripes* wanted to find out what would happen to the pin-up and its progeny after the war was over, staff writer Roy Craft went after the subject in the June 3, 1945 issue, saying: "In World War II, the Pin-Ups—featuring legs, bosoms, and exotic coiffures—have achieved their greatest and perhaps ultimate stature.

"With a peculiar combination of forthrightness and affectionate good taste, they combine in their posture and setting the American ideal of Sweethearts Glorified. Many a husband and father who wouldn't get within ten feet of a babe while doing his military chores overseas has been known to paper the inside of his footlocker with photographs of Alexis Smith.

"A survey of personnel in this theater [Europe], representing a cross

The 95th BG's whimsical *Ikky Poo*.

Quite often both sides of an aircraft were used to give a reverse view of the same piece of nose art. *Tropical Trollop,* a B-24 attached to the Seventh Air Force, is seen here from both sides at Kwajelein, Marshall Islands, in July 1944.

31

Calamity Jane, with a horse's head virtually identical to her sister ship *The Mustang* of the 43rd and 19th Bomb Groups, racked up an outstanding record in the early days of the war in New Guinea. *Boeing*

Upper left
Flying out of Port Moresby, New Guinea, with the 63rd BS, 43rd BG, Flying Fort *Panama Hattie* was named after the Cole Porter movie musical starring Ann Southern, Red Skelton, and Lena Horne. *Boeing*

Satan's Lady was a brand-new B–17G when assigned to the 369th BS, 306th BG crew of Loy F. Peterson in October 1943. Peterson, whose original B–17F was named *Satan's Mistress,* thought the new name made sense. He recalled that *Lady* became known as a lucky ship and that crews wanted her on their last missions. He flew her on D-day and on his last mission nine days later. According to crew chief Harry Tzipowitz she flew until the end of the war, logging "112 missions without a mechanical failure and always came back on four engines. She was shot quite a bit but with a lot of patching up and repairs it was off to another mission. Numerous crews finished their 25th mission on her and no one ever got wounded to get a Purple Heart. Also, many copilots were checked out as pilots on her and she was one of the first planes over Germany." *Loy F. Peterson*

section of the Air Forces, Ground Forces, and Service Forces and embracing all military grades, reveals that the boys go for Pin-Ups because (and this is significant) *they like to look at them*!"

But what of the postwar future? Could returning GIs put their favorite gals and photos of nose art on their walls and "expect the Little Woman to approve"? *The Stars and Stripes'* New York Bureau went to George Gallup, who sent his pollsters out to ask women across the nation. The result was 52 percent yes, 46 percent no, and 2 percent undecided. However, when the veterans themselves asked, they said the general attitude could best be summed up with, "He damn' well better not!"

Craft finished the article by saying it was a safe bet this morale-boosting "phenomenon of World War II will quietly slip back into the movie magazines and gentlemen's style magazines when the last shot has been fired." That turned out to be the case . . . until the next war heated up five years later.

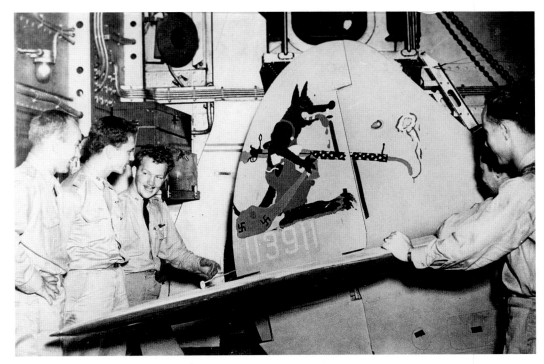

Rudder art was quite common among the USAAF P–40s which fought in North Africa. This P–40F below decks on the USS *Ranger* during Operation Torch is admired by army and navy pilots. *James H. Farmer*

When the "Green Dragons" of the 405th BS, 38th BG transitioned from B–25s into A–26 Invaders, their famous nose markings were applied as well. *Merle Olmsted via James H. Farmer*

In North Africa, P–40 units used large renditions of their squadron insignia as nose art. When 86th FS personnel put a captured Ju 88 back into flying condition, they could not resist decorating it appropriately. *USAF via NASM*

33

This Eighth Air Force B-24 *You're Safe At Home* expressed a genuine bomber crew sentiment through use of a well-known baseball phrase. *Mark H. Brown via USAFA*

Quite often the addition of armor plate, as on this Eighth AF B-24J, eliminated part of the nose art. There was so little time to catch up with things between missions that it would seldom be replaced. *Mark H. Brown via USAFA*

With a set of feather fans taking the place of the first name, *Merchant* was a stunning example of 493rd Bomb Group artistry. *Mark H. Brown via USAFA*

Big Dealer was a B–24 of the 493rd Bomb Group. *Mark H. Brown via USAFA*

A favorite with GIs across the world was Sad Sack, the cartoon soldier who embodied army life at the lower ranks. This adaptation of him carrying a massive crate strapped to his back is an astute comment on the mission of this Air Transport Command C–47 in England. *Mark H. Brown via USAFA*

The Joker lost some of its art to increased armor plate, but that didn't lessen its colorful impact when flying with the Eighth AF. *Mark H. Brown via USAFA*

With a rabbit, four-leaf clover, and a horseshoe, clearly the crew of *Dee Luck* wanted all they could get when flying this

490th Bomb Group Liberator. *Mark H. Brown via USAFA*

By the end of the war, 447th BG Fort *D-Day Doll* had flown seventy-nine missions. The plane was flown back to the States only to be cut up for scrap at Kingman, Arizona. *Mark H. Brown via USAFA*

Sgt. Frank Stevens, a welding and sheet-metal shop man with the 100th Bomb Group, created a number of fine nose art paintings, among them *Mason And Dixon*, which was loosely named for pilot Buck Mason and navigator Bill Dishion. *Mark H. Brown via USAFA*

Shark mouths were nothing new during World War II, having shown up during the previous big war. This No. 112 Squadron, RAF, Kittyhawk taxis across the North African desert with the help of the ground crewman on the wing. It was this unit's fierce markings that inspired Chennault's Flying Tigers to so decorate their Curtiss fighters. *Frank F. Smith*

Pierce W. McKennon flew a number of fighters with the 4th Fighter Group and *Ridge Runner III* was among the last, seen here at Debden, England, in April 1945. *Joseph B. Sills*

Capt. Dick Perley with his *Kandy K II* at Toul-Ochey Airfield near Nancy, France, in the spring of 1945. Sgt. Lester L. Schaufler, 318th FS nose artist, painted most of the unit's Thunderbolts, including Perley's, making the 50th FG stand out wherever it went. *Richard H. Perley*

An armorer cleans one of the .50 caliber machine guns from a 56th FG Thunderbolt at Boxted, England. *Mark H. Brown via USAFA*

Pilot Walter E. Zurney and crew chief Carl Beluchu in front of their *Taffy,* a P–38J attached to the 97th FS, 82nd FG at Foggia, Italy, in 1944. Zurney transferred from B–24s to fly Lightnings, something many bomber pilots had wanted to do. *Walter E. Zurney*

Jumpin' Jacques, the favorite P–51D of Jacques Young, 3rd Squadron, 3rd Air Commando Group, during sunset at Gabu Strip, Luzon, Philippines, in June 1945. Bugs Bunny was painted on the side yelling the word, "Halt!" The large theater black, white, and black recognition bands can be seen on the wings and fuselage. *Jacques Young*

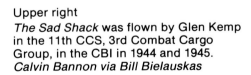

Loddie Roeder's *Noshak Murph,* 10th CCS, 3rd CCG at Muse, Burma, in March 1945. *Calvin Bannon via Bill Bielauskas*

Upper right
The Sad Shack was flown by Glen Kemp in the 11th CCS, 3rd Combat Cargo Group, in the CBI in 1944 and 1945. *Calvin Bannon via Bill Bielauskas*

General Sultan traveled around the CBI in a C–47 that carried an appropriate piece of nose art. Here, *Sultan's Magic Carpet* sits at Bhamo, Burma, May 1945. *Calvin Bannon via Bill Bielauskas*

While commanding the 475th Fighter Group in the Pacific, Col. Charles H. MacDonald flew a series of P-38s, all named *Putt Putt Maru*. In this photo, legendary pilot Charles A. Lindbergh sits in the cockpit prior to taxiing out on a mission with the 475th during 1944. *John L. Trease via Lawrence Hickey*

Donald Firoved and Ralph Francis, ground crew for Bill Skinner's 308th FS, 31st FG *Lonesome Polecat,* wait for mission start time at Castel Volturno, Italy, in March 1944. American pilots in the 31st and 52nd FGs loved their reverse Lend Lease Spitfires and had mixed emotions about trading them in for P-51s. *William J. Skinner*

Clark's Little Pill leads a line of early Eighth Air Force B-26 Marauders for takeoff from England, 1943. USAF/NASM

Bathtub Bessie was a B-24D operating out of North Africa in 1943. *William J. Skinner*

Cpl. Ruby Newell, a 3rd Bomb Division staff worker, was selected as the most beautiful WAC in the ETO through a contest in *Stars And Stripes,* resulting in nose art on several aircraft from P-51s to B-17s. Newell is standing next to one of her namesakes, *Ruby's Raiders,* a 385th BG B-17G painted by Corporal Ploss. Newell died in February 1981 and was buried in the national cemetery at March AFB, California. *Clark B. Rollins, Jr.*

Shack Rat sits at its 56th Fighter Group hardstand, Boxted, England. *Mark H. Brown via USAFA*

Upper left
The B–25 *Sunday Punch* was known for giving just that, particularly in later strafing versions. Numerous .50 caliber machine guns and even a 75 mm cannon were mounted in the nose. The .50s have been fired, as evidenced by the gunpowder flash marks. *Via Frank F. Smith*

Though more rare, nose art was applied to transports, as seen on *Fire Fly,* which also carried the insignia of Troop Carrier Command. *USAF via Dana Bell*

Next page
A 56th FG P–47D, *Belle Of Belmont,* taxies out at Boxted, England, in 1944 for a long-range escort mission. *Mark H. Brown via USAFA*

Maj. Milton Joel's *Flying Wolf* at its 55th Fighter Group base, Nuthampstead, England, on November 18, 1943. As nose artist Sgt. Robert T. Sand recalled, "While still at Paine Field, Washington (or possibly Pendleton Field), I designed this emblem (borrowing a little from Walt Disney) for a squadron party, at Milton Joel's request. At Nuthampstead he adopted this design for his own emblem. Shortly after this picture was taken the squadron had one of its most unhappy days when Milton Joel, Lieutenant Albino, Lieutenant Garvin and Lieutenant Carrol were lost in action. Joel was rumored to have actually escaped from Europe and returned to England or the U.S. but I never heard anything to substantiate this rumor. *Robert T. Sand*

Sgt. Robert T. Sand painted the nose art on Col. Jack Jenkins' 55th FG P–38 *Texas Ranger*. The missing rope shows this not to be Jenkins' first P–38, since the gun bay door was removed after at least two belly-landings and transferred to subsequent fighters. Sand was unable to keep up and repaint the rope, a task finally undertaken by another ground crewman. *Robert T. Sand*

As aircraft were gathered for the scrapper's torch, nose art such as *Gambler's Luck* still drew attention, even down to the final moment.

Awaiting the smelter in the American desert, this pathfinder Liberator still carries a massive representation of the Fourteenth Air Force stylized Flying Tiger, a carryover from Claire Chennault's days as founder of the American Volunteer Group.

Maj. Chuck Sweeney's *The Great Artiste,* loaded with blast gauges and other measurement devices, served as the instrument aircraft for the 509th Composite Group atomic strike on Hiroshima. *Frank F. Smith*

Erotic Edna was one of the 75 mm cannon-equipped B-25H Mitchells with Phil Cochran's 1st Air Commando Group in the CBI during 1944. *R. T. Smith*

When Flying Tiger ace Robert T. Smith came home he picked up his commission with the AAF and headed back to China for another combat tour, this time with the 1st Air Commando Group. Here, he stands in front of his 1st ACG P-51A, *Barbie. R. T. Smith*

Though the nost art of the 1st Air Commando Group's P–51A Mustangs was relatively simple, the pilots were known for flying complex missions in the CBI theater. *R. T. Smith*

Ninth Air Force B–26B *Flak Bait* flew 202 missions with the 449th BS, 322nd BG from the summer of 1943 to the end of the war in April 1945. No other American aircraft equaled that record. In spite of the Martin's ability to make it back each time, it took hundreds of flak hits, thus earning its name. The proud bomber still exists today as a part of the National Air and Space Museum. *C. F. McClain*

Rat Poison, a 386th BG Marauder, sits at its French base in 1944. One of the high-mission aircraft in the Group, it earned the respect of air and ground crew alike. Lt. John Meyers, pilot of *La Paloma,* stands in front of the bomber. *John H. Meyers/NASM*

A Fifth Air Force B-25J showing signs of wear still carries its well-maintained nose art. *Frank F. Smith*

The nose art on *Miss Judy,* a 462nd BG Superfortress which reached Tinian, in the S. Marianas, in June 1945, was one of many American machines around the world that expressed obvious feelings toward the enemy in cartoon form. *Frank F. Smith*

Heading out over the Mediterranean is 320th BG Marauder *Thumper II. Joseph S. Kingsbury*

An Angel carrying a Tommy gun with a lantern hung on the barrel reflects this black Liberator's job of night pathfinding and secret missions. Noting the mission score on the side, it is sad to see the B-24 outlast the war only to be photographed at one of the many boneyards in 1948, awaiting the smelter.

Some of the most lavish mural nose art of the war was painted on 43rd BG Liberators at Ie Shima in the Pacific in 1945 by an artist named Bartigan. *Mabel's Labels* is shown at Kingman, Arizona, in 1947 during its last days. Bartigan was probably most famous for painting *The Dragon And His Tail,* though he also created *It Ain't So Funny, Last Horizon, Michigan,* and *Cocktail Hour.*

The crew of 320th BG Marauder *Sandra Lee* poses for a publicity shot.

RAF Bomber Command took heavy losses throughout the war but aircraft such as *Friday The 13th,* a Handley Page Halifax III, managed to rack up numerous missions and still come home. When the aircraft was scrapped, the nose art was snipped out and is now on display in London at the Imperial War Museum. *Edward B. Richie*

Squadron artists often came up with some very original cartoon art, as seen on this B-24 *Hell's Belle. Lucky Stevens*

Upper right and right
Some nose art characters were painted on many individual aircraft in many areas across the globe. *Superstitious Aloysius* was a popular good-luck elf who carried just about every charm known to man, including a wishbone, horseshoe, four-leaf clover, tied string (on his nose), and rabbit's foot while crossing his fingers. These examples in the Eighth Air Force show crews wanted all the luck they could get. *Mark H. Brown via USAFA*

Double Trouble was an early B–17F attached to the 94th BG. *Mark H. Brown via USAFA*

Lady From Hell was an Eighth AF B–24. *Mark H. Brown via USAFA*

Running up on the hardstand before a mission, *Cash & Carrie* is warmed up by the ground crew. *Mark H. Brown via USAFA*

Laden Maid was assigned to the 786th BS, 466th BG from February to September 1944 and was salvaged after the war ended. *John W. Sweeney via Bill Bielauskas*

This B-24D, *Sure Pop,* had at least two messages on the nose about the certainty of V for victory, one in Morse code. *Lucky Stevens*

Miss Alaynious was an early Eighth AF P-47. *Mark H. Brown via USAFA*

Princess Pat's 458th BG artist was able to cope with the addition of armor plate while still managing to place personal names at various stations, including the fairing between the front turret and bombardier's position. *John M. Campbell*

Tepee Time Gal flew with the 753rd BS, 455th BG, Fifteenth AF in 1944 and 1945. *Mike McCleskey via Will Addison*

Upper left
Lieutenant Leder, 39th FS, 35th FG, seems fairly happy with the door art on his P–39 at Port Moresby, New Guinea, 1942. *John Stanaway*

Both pilot and crew chief seem to be getting a kick out of what *Grapefruit's Gator* is doing to Hitler. *Larry Davis*

Joe Origlio painted a number of pieces on 307th BG B–24s, including *Indian Thummer. 307th BG Assn. via James M. Kendall*

Frances Darling looks as if she has clothes on, but a closer inspection reveals quite a bit more. *Larry Davis*

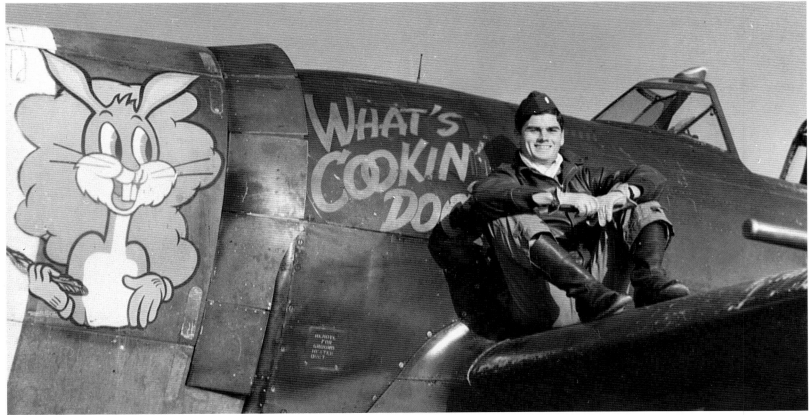

Bugs Bunny was a constant favorite, though *What's Cookin' Doc?* doesn't quite have the wise-cracking rabbit's famous phrase right. *Larry Davis*

Royal Nose Art

Though World War II nose art was predominantly an American phenomenon, crews from Britain, Canada, Australia, New Zealand and South Africa applied a substantial amount of personalized art to their aircraft. Often inspired by their own national symbols, artists were still, for the most part, drawn to the Petty and Varga Girls from *Esquire* or their own imagined females.

Right
Copied from a British cartoon strip extremely popular with the military services, the nose art on Vickers Wellington *Jane* was cut out by the Germans as a trophy after the bomber was downed on June 21, 1942, by night fighter pilot Prinz zur Lippe-Weissenfeld. This was his twenty-seventh kill. *George Petersen*

A Halifax of No. 425 Squadron, *The Fiery Queen,* on May 10, 1944. *Canadian EAVC*

Hi Toots was a Mk. II Mosquito which flew with No. 418 Squadron, RCAF in March 1944 as a day and night intruder. The squadron's tally of 178 enemy aircraft and 79.5 V–1 flying bombs made it the top-scoring unit of the RCAF. *Canadian EAVC*

Royal Nose Art

Another Halifax from No. 425 Squadron, *Pistol Packing Peggy,* on April 17, 1944. *Canadian EAVC*

Fannin' Fanny, a No. 427 Squadron Lancaster, April 4, 1945. *Canadian EAVC*

No. 159 Squadron Liberator *Lady X* was flown by Sam Kinnear's crew from Digri, India, in 1945. *Canadian EAVC*

The song that inspired the art for this No. 432 Squadron Halifax, *Pistol Packin' Mama,* made its way across every theater to become one of the most common nose art names of the war. *Canadian EAVC*

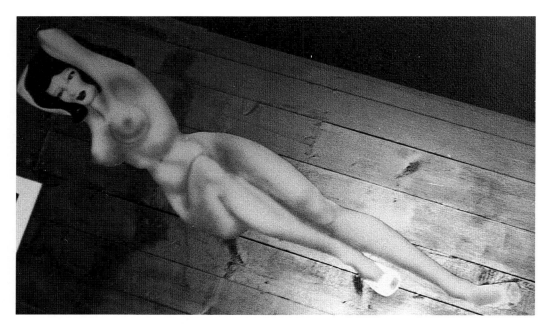

Unit nose artists were called upon to decorate numerous things other than aircraft, including jackets, leather patches, mess halls, and the insides of bars and recreation rooms, as can be seen here.

Nilan Jones, talented artist with the 352nd FG, poses with some of his creations that decorated group buildings. His nose art was just as eye catching. *Jones via Samuel L. Sox, Jr.*

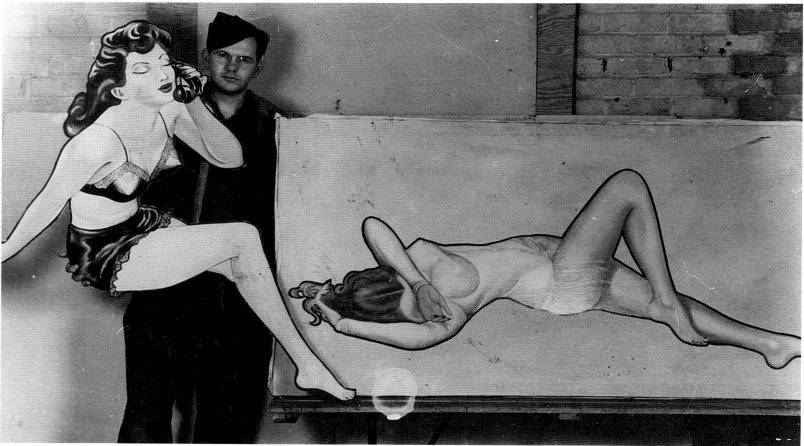

Hells-Belles are getting an intense briefing from their boss. *Mark H. Brown via USAFA*

Zack Mosely, creator of "Smilin' Jack," sent a possible squadron insignia for the 328th FS, 352nd FG but it was not accepted by the AAF. That didn't stop pilot Bill Schwenke from adopting the art for his P–47. Both pilot and aircraft were lost on March 11, 1944. *Dick DeBruin via Samuel L. Sox, Jr.*

Lower right
When Wright Field test pilot Gus Lundquist bellied-in the AAF experimental long-range Spitfire IX at BW8 in Greenland on the way to England, he managed to set it down on full drop tanks without extreme damage. Before leaving on a B–25 for England to get spare parts from Supermarine, Lundquist was approached by Sergeant Petta, one of the station mechanics, and asked if he minded Petta painting some nose art on the Spit. Lundquist said fine and one week later, arriving with his parts on a B–17, he saw this incredible representation of one of George Petty's more popular *Esquire* creations. Lundquist had Tolly Hello added (he later married Tolly), repaired the Spit and continued on to England. At each stop in Iceland, Scotland, and finally Boscombe Down, where it was turned over to the RAF, the Spitfire was greatly admired. The aircraft did not last long, however, since the British considered the extensive addition of internal fuel tanks the ruin of a perfectly good flying machine. Its fine handling characteristics had disappeared, though it could fly quite far. When the Spit was scrapped, the cowling was removed and hung over the bar at the Boscombe Down Officer's Mess. Lundquist talked Eighth AF Fighter Command CO Gen. Bill Kepner into letting him join the 352nd FG for a combat tour. He was shot down twenty-seven hours later to become one of the very few, if not the only, AAF test pilot POW. *Gus Lundquist via Samuel L. Sox, Jr.*

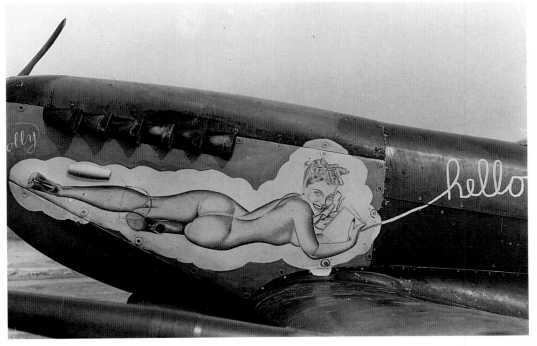

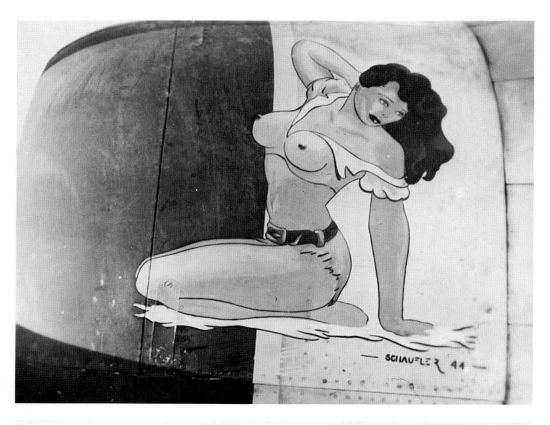

Another Les Schaufler lovely on the cowl of a 50th FG P-47. *Via Gil Burns*

Upper left
Les Schaufler nose art on Bernie Knoll's Thunderbolt. The name *Scanty Pants* adorned the fuselage. *Bernie Knoll via Gil Burns*

Les Schaufler painted *Mrs. D* exactly like a pinup in the December 1944 military edition of *Esquire. Via Gil Burns*

A rare example of wartime Luftwaffe aircraft art on the tail of an He 111 early in the war. *George Petersen*

Upper right
Luftwaffe ace Maj. Heinz Bär holds the mascot which matches the crest on his Messerschmitt 109. *Peter Petrick*

Japanese aircraft featured very little embellished art during World War II, until late in the conflict when Army Air Force units in particular had unit flashes applied to the rear fuselage and vertical tail surfaces. This Dinah reconnaissance aircraft, shot down by Fourteenth Air Force fighters over China, exhibits a large, stylized tiger which has clearly caught the attention of AAF personnel. *USAF*

Anna Belle–Just A Friend with the Seventh AF's 413th FG in the Pacific. *Via W. E. Scarborough*

Sitting in the Pacific island heat doesn't seem to bother 35th FS, 8th FG P-38 Lightning *G.I. Miss U. Via W. E. Scarborough*

As the 8th FG moved up the line with the Fifth AF advances, 35th FS Lightning *So Inviting* flew from the Philippines until mid–1945 when the squadron moved to Ie Shima. *Via W. E. Scarborough*

The 8th FG's *Miss Cheri* had nose art based on one of Alberto Vargas' more popular *Esquire* girls. *Via W. E. Scarborough*

Though unnamed, the nose art on this 80th FS Headhunter P–38 probably didn't need a name to attract attention. *Via W. E. Scarborough*

Upper left
Nose artist Eldon T. Gladden of the 6th Night Fighter Squadron was known across the Seventh AF's Pacific island bases for creations such as *The Virgin Widow*. *Edward T. Donnelly via Steve Birdsall*

Chow Hound Junior was a stripped-down B–25D "fat cat" used by the 345th BG to make provisions runs and transport flights from May to July 1945. Here it sits at Clark Field in the Philippines around June 1945. *Maury Eppstein via Steve Birdsall*

Frank Spangler painted a number of outstanding pieces of nose art on 394th BG Marauders in France with the Ninth AF, including *Miss Manookie, Round Too!,* and *Sure Go For No Dough. Joe LeMoure via Steve Birdsall*

Crew chief Sgt. Paul Fast stands with his 584th BS, 394th BG Marauder *Ish-Tak-Ha-Ba,* which was named by the plane's original pilot, Lt. Martin Harter of Sleepy Eye, Minnesota. The English language equivalent for the Indian name was sleepy eye. On its 101st mission, the B–26 hit and sheared off a telephone pole. The damaged bomber brought its crew home and landed with 11 ft. of pole sticking out of the wing. *Paul E. Fast via Steve Birdsall*

The 548th NFS had a talented nose artist whose last name was Miozzi. His *Lady In The Dark,* one of the better known P–61s, was stylized after Vargas' famous one-armed girl from the June 1943 *Esquire* gatefold, and the squadron insignia was painted next to her. *USMC via James H. Farmer*

Blue Devil, a P–51C, sits at Furth, Germany, in 1945. *Chris Goodman via Norm Taylor*

One advantage of flying a Lightning, whether a fighter or a reconnaissance version, was three noses for the application of nose art. This 34th PhS F–5E at Haguenau, France, in the summer of 1945 carries something on just about every available surface. *Chris Goodman via Norm Taylor*

A'Peel'N Baby of the 34th PhS at Haguenau, France, in the fall of 1944. *Chris Goodman via Norm Taylor*

Though virtually unknown, 376th BG B–24D *Wongo Wongo!* is one of the most significant combat aircraft of World War II. Flown by Brian Flavelle's crew during the August 1, 1943, low-level mission to Ploesti, Romania, the Liberator crashed into the sea outboard to the target. In the subsequent official mission summaries it was listed as carrying the lead navigator on the mission, which resulted in the other aircraft making the wrong turn, thus fouling up the timing over the target which caused the groups to bomb out of sequence. This single error was blamed for the failure of the mission. In reality, *Wongo Wongo!* was the eighth aircraft back in the 379th formation, and the navigation failure made by the lead element was blamed on the loss of Flavelle's crew to cover up the actual lead navigator's failure. Every historical account written since then, except for researcher Tom Davidson's single article published in the late 1970s, has claimed *Wongo Wongo!* carried the lead navigator. *USAF via Tom Davidson*

Milt Caniff and Al Capp: Happily Self Drafted

Innumerable pieces of wartime nose art were based on the comic strip characters created by Milt Caniff and Al Capp—particularly their well endowed women. Both of them were very patriotic and both were 4F (unfit for military service), Caniff due to chronic phlebitis and Capp due to a leg amputation. Caniff was actually drafted twice, reported eagerly, and was promptly thrown back out. They led such active lives until their deaths in the 1980s that few suspected there was anything wrong with them at all.

During World War II they, along with many other artistic professionals such as Herblock and Sgt. George Baker (creator of "Sad Sack"), "drafted" themselves and turned their talents toward serving Uncle Sam by donating artwork. When Capp and Caniff first volunteered they were put to work doing cautionary posters about venereal disease but Caniff's were turned down because the bad girls were too good looking and Capp's were sent back because he overplayed it.

Capp's Dogpatch characters from "Li'l Abner" soon started showing up on all types of vehicles across all nationalities. However, they found their greatest expression when entire fighter or bomber units would paint his hillbillys on each aircraft in suc-

Col. Dave Schilling, CO of the 56th FG, just before take-off in company of a wingman at Boxted, England. His P–47 *Hairless Joe* was one of several group Thunderbolts whose nose art was based on Al Capp's "Li'l Abner" comic strip. *Mark H. Brown via USAFA*

Milt Caniff and Al Capp: Happily Self Drafted

Al Capp's Moonbeam McSwine decorates this 5th Emergency Rescue Squadron P–47 based at Boxted, England, along with the 56th FG. The 56th had an entire series of nose art creations based on Al Capp's "Li'l Abner," and the same artist painted this one. *Mark H. Brown via USAFA*

Lt. Lester Twigg stands in front of his *Moonshine McSwine* on the hard coral strip at Iwo Jima. The 47th FS of the 15th FG were known as the "Dogpatchers," and they adopted the entire line of Capp characters to decorate their Seventh AF Mustangs. *John W. Lambert*

Right and following page
The Mosquitos of No. 418 Squadron, RCAF, adopted Capp's characters as well, painting them in succession on their fast intruder fighters. *Li'l Abner, Black Rufe,* and *Cousin Jake* were all No. 418 Squadron Mosquitos photographed at Hurn on July 22, 1944. *Canadian EAVC*

Milt Caniff and Al Capp: Happily Self Drafted

cession until the entire pantheon was flying against the enemy.

Caniff, best known for "Terry and the Pirates," offered to create a comic strip just for the troops, which would appear in the 3,000 papers within the Army's Camp Newspaper Service. Getting no money for what became "Male Call," Caniff drew the daily strip in addition to "Terry" which came out seven days a week. It was an incredible output by any standard.

The characters most duplicated from "Terry" were the all-American gal Burma, one of her alter egos, Madame Shoo Shoo, and the unbelieveable Dragon Lady. When "Male Call" started circulating in 1942 the incredible Miss Lace showed up inside, much to the delight of GIs around the world. As Caniff remembered, "When I fashioned Miss Lace, I wanted someone who was the opposite of Burma, so right away, I gave her black hair. I viewed her as innocent but sexy as hell—much more so than the standard of the day. I was on pioneering ground here, because I wanted her to have 'it' without being overt. . . .

"I didn't base Lace on any movie stars. She was the visualization of an idea, a point of view. It was as if she was a genie, a waif, who appeared in your dreams. When she turned the tables on some hot pants GI, or the hot pants colonel for that matter, it was fun. It was a wish fulfillment for the readers. She was always there, always available, and yet *not* available. The whole thing hung on the point of view of the American GI, the American guy suddenly dumped in a place he'd never heard of before. What he's really thinking about is the girl back home, not the tavern wench near the air base in England. That's for officers anyway. So all he can think about is miss so and so back home. There are a number of kissing scenes in the strips, which was the kind of thing that most guys would have loved to have happened. But they never expected it to happen in reality, and so that's where the dreams came in. It was a wish fulfillment, and in a way, it was in the nature of a two minute furlough

Milt Caniff and Al Capp: Happily Self Drafted

back home for the guys when they read the strip."

Reaction to "Male Call" was overwhelming and Caniff got a *lot* of fan mail about Miss Lace, including requests for large drawings of the women which could be used as models for nose art. The strip lasted through the war, then was withdrawn when the troops got home.

Permission to quote Milton Caniff was generously given by Kitchen Sink Press, No. 2 Swamp Rd., Princeton, WI 54968. The entire wartime run of "Male Call" may be purchased from Kitchen Sink as a book for $11.95 plus $2.00 shipping.

Lined up for take-off at Boxted, England, Thunderbolts of the 63rd FS, 56th FG are about to launch a long range escort mission. *Amaposa II* was Russell Westfall's second assigned Thunderbolt with nose art based on an Al Capp comic strip Indian. *Mark H. Brown via USAFA*

Milt Caniff and Al Capp: Happily Self Drafted

Capt. Bull Durham, 307th BG intelligence officer, with *Burma,* named for Milton Caniff's "Terry and the Pirates" character. *307th BG Assn. via James M. Kendall*

One of the numerous personal pieces of art done by Milt Caniff for servicemen during the war, this one of the slinky Dragon Lady from "Terry and the Pirates." *Copyright Milton Caniff*

Milt Caniff and Al Capp: Happily Self Drafted

The nose artist for this 505th BG B-29 took a bit more liberty with the original Caniff Dragon Lady.

The long fuselage of this 489th BG Superfortress was ideal to present the striking form of Milton Caniff's envied GI favorite. *Miss Lace* flew forty-nine consecutive missions without an abort. *Edward T. Donnelly via Steve Birdsall*

Milt Caniff and Al Capp: Happily Self Drafted

This 444th BG crew decided to name their B-29 *Male Call* after Milt Caniff's GI comic strip rather than the star character Miss Lace, painted on the side.

A Bit Of Lace was a B-25 in the CBI theater. Thornton W. Rose via Bill Bielauskas

Navy automatic pilot specialist Hal Olsen was assigned to Instrument Trailer Group 3 with CASU–44 when he arrived on Tinian. Bringing oil paints and brushes with the intention of painting the local scenery, he was soon discovered by the local PB4Y Privateer squadrons and began painting nose art. The results were legendary across the theater with such creations as *Miss Lottatail, Pistol Packin' Mama III, Lady Luck, Indian Made, Sleepytime Gal*, and *Easy Maid*. In the photo, Olsen is putting the finishing touches on *Accentuate The Positive. Will Addison*

Upper right
Lady, a Seventh AF B–24 at Kwajalein Atoll in July 1944, typifies one of the most popular of all the Varga Girls, a gatefold from the October 1943 issue of *Esquire*. She appeared on countless aircraft through the end of the war. *Will Addison*

Another of the more popular Varga Girls transferred from *Esquire* to aircraft was the January 1944 calendar girl—by the end of the war she was painted on everything from this B–24 to Jeeps. *Will Addison*

Sgt. Duane Bryers painted a significant number of 487th BG Liberators in England, including *Purty Baby*. Mark H. Brown via USAFA

Pacific Liberator *After Hours* sits on Ie Shima toward the end of the war looking as good as ever. *Via W. E. Scarborough*

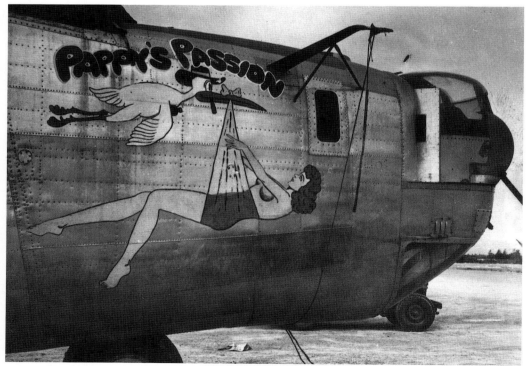

Up the creek without a paddle seems to explain the predicament felt by the crew of B–24 *S.O.L. Mark H. Brown via USAFA*

Left

The 90th BG's *Pappy's Passion* put in a long history of bombing missions over the Pacific with the Fifth AF. *Via W. E. Scarborough*

The Seventh AF's 30th BG exhibited a series of outstanding nose art paintings during the last year of the war. *Warren Coughlin via Steve Birdsall*

Another of nose artist Bartigan's huge 43rd BG B–24 murals. *Via W. E. Scarborough*

The 98th BG Liberator *Cielito Lindo* was one of numerous wartime aircraft that based nose art on George Petty's girl on a swing. *Australian War Memorial via Steve Birdsall*

The 30th BG crew of *The Captain And The Kids* emulates their Liberator's nose art, patterned after the popular comic strip "The Katzenjammer Kids." *John Gleason via Steve Birdsall*

The 498th BG's *Tanaka Termite* flew a total of sixty missions before being sent home as war weary in August 1945. The Group artist, Hernandez, created what some consider to be the finest nose art of the war. *Edward T. Donnelly via Steve Birdsall*

Lucky 'Leven of the 498th BG had the right name. Lt. Barton Yount and crew took *'Leven* on the first Tokyo mission, November 24, 1944, and it flew its sixtieth mission on August 14, 1945, the day before the war ended. *Edward T. Donnelly via Steve Birdsall*

The 498th BG inherited *Heavenly Body* from the 505th Group in January 1945. The fighter was so badly shot up on April 1 that it was sent to the Guam Air Depot and lost to the unit. *Edward T. Donnelly via Steve Birdsall*

Lt. William Kelly's *Lucky Irish,* 497th BG, was painted by John Albright. *Edward T. Donnelly via Steve Birdsall*

The 504th BG's *Lucky Lady.*

Phony Express gives a good idea of just how much room a talented artist had to play with if he had the time. *Ron Witt*

Upper left
A 3rd Photo Recon Squadron F-13A, the photo recce version of the B-29, named *Poison Ivy,* derived from crew chief Sergeant Ivey. *Bob Watson via Steve Birdsall*

Giving photo F-13s names keyed to their mission was common, such as *Double Exposure,* a 3rd Photo Squadron aircraft

with art based on the February 1942 Vargas *Esquire* gatefold. *Bob Watson via Steve Birdsall*

Lt. Ralph DeVore's 509th Composite Group atomic strike Superfortress *Next Objective,* which carried the markings of the 444th BG to disguise its mission. *John Dulin via Steve Birdsall*

Marine Pfc. Randall "Bud" Sprenger painted the nost art on 479th BG Capt. Pershing Yon's *Coral Queen*. With the 3rd Battalion, Tenth Marines, Sprenger had an extensive art background with the Curtis Candy Company as a sign painter. He usually got $175 and whiskey for each nose art job. *USMC via Steve Birdsall*

Don Allen (right) and Jerry Byrge pose in front of their P-51, *Blondie*. Allen painted some of the best nose art of World War II onto the noses of the 4th FG's Thunderbolts and Mustangs. *Don Allen*

Chapter 4

Cowling for Canvas

The Nose Artists

By the sheer numbers of men and women who served in World War II, the availability of talented artists to decorate weapons of war was bound to be high. Virtually every unit on the line was able to come up with someone who could translate impersonal machines into cherished talismans through brush and palette.

Unfortunately, most of these wartime artistic wizards have remained in obscurity without recognition for their beloved contributions. Few signed their work and, almost without exception, their paintings were created in off-duty hours, even at night, after working hard on the line or flying combat. Paints, brushes, solvents, and other materials were often hard to come by, particularly in the Pacific, but ingenuity and inexhaustible enthusiasm overcame even the most difficult of circumstances. The last thing they worried about was recognition.

Considering the United States alone built 300,000 aircraft in World War II, the number of nose artists across the globe will never be known. Each one deserves credit and to single out just a few seems unfair to the rest. Nevertheless, here are some of the magicians who used noses and cowlings for canvas, propelling air crews into combat with the confidence that came from knowing they were riding a good and true ship.

Donald E. Allen, *4th Fighter Group*
Ever since Don Allen can remember, he has loved being an artist. From kindergarten on, teachers would catch him drawing in the margins and inside the covers of his books. In high school he managed to take five classes of art-related subjects during the day and still serve as a set designer and builder for the school plays.

After debating about becoming an architect, Allen enrolled for a full four-year art program in the Cleveland School of Art, graduating in 1941 with a major in illustration and a drafting job to start his career. Then came Pearl Harbor; by February 1942, Private Allen was in the Army. The closest he could come to locating an artist's job was in the camouflage section at Fort Belvoir, Virginia, but he could never seem to find an office to apply for it. Though he was not mechanically minded in the least, Allen's aptitude tests led to his assignment to USAAF engine and airframe mechanic's school at Sheppard Field, Texas.

During the thirteen-week course, Allen remembers that the deafening roar of aircraft engines was constant; at least one engine was running on one of the twenty stands at all times while he learned the basics of the AT-6 and P-40. His class was then shipped to Seattle for B-17 school but upon completion they were sent back across country, held "prisoner" in an Atlantic City hotel for three weeks, then marched aboard the *Queen Elizabeth* to cross the Atlantic for England. As was typical during wartime, the whole group was assigned the very opposite of what they'd trained for. After three weeks at Atcham, they were transferred to Debden and began learning how to take care of the 4th Fighter Group's Spitfires from the British crews on the field. The few months on British rations were miserable, but stopping for tea time each day had its benefits.

My Achin' Back was a common sentiment among pilots after long escort missions. Don Allen captured it beautifully on this 334th FS, 4th FG Mustang. *Larry Hendel*

Don Allen created *Miss Plainfield* for Lt. Spiros "Steve" Pisanos. *Leo Schmidt via Tom Ivie*

Crew chief S.Sgt. Donald E. Allen with Lt. Clarence L. Boretsky's *Meg*. Allen's lettering of names was very distinctive. *Don Allen*

By March 1943 the 4th had transitioned to P–47 Thunderbolts and Private Allen was assigned to the 334th Fighter Squadron as crew chief to the fighter shared by Spiros N. "Steve" Pisanos and Aubrey Stanhope. When Pisanos got his own P–47, Allen stayed with Stanhope, resulting in Allen's first nose art creation. According to Allen, the painting was a collaboration: "As I recall it was his choice to have a black panther and I added the fleur-de-lis to reflect Lieutenant Stanhope's French background. He was the son of an American father and French mother, born in France and living there as an American citizen until 1940 . . . he could barely speak English. This piece of art really started the ball rolling—once it was on one plane, other pilots wanted something on theirs too."

When Stanhope was transferred to another squadron with his P–47, Allen became crew chief for Vic France, who wanted *Miss Dallas* painted on the cowling. One of Allen's two favorite creations, it was hardly finished when Lt. Col. Chesley Peterson borrowed the P–47 to lead the group. *Miss Dallas* was hit by flak in the engine, blowing off the entire top of the cowling. Peterson bailed out into the English Channel. When France got a new Thunderbolt, Allen repainted the art and then reprised it yet again when the 4th Fighter Group was re-equipped with Mustangs.

"I repeated several pieces of nose art," recalled Allen, "onto Mustangs, including *Boise Bee* [for Duane Beeson], *Ill Wind* [for Nick Megura], *Salem Representative* [for Ralph

Several pieces of Don Allen's nose art were recreated when the 4th FG transitioned to Mustangs. *Ill Wind?* was painted on Nick Megura's fighters, though the art itself was changed a bit. *Leo Schmidt via Tom Ivie*

Hofer]. I figure I did something like thirty-nine pieces of nose art and sixteen names alone when pilots didn't want an illustration.

"Painting materials were always a bug-a-boo. I'd go up to the hangar to borrow the very limited colors used in painting to Army specs—blue, red, zinc chromate primer, black and others. I'd chisel paint from them and others here and there, including lacquer which was so terrible to brush

Don Allen's working sketch for Nick Megura's *Ill Wind?*. Don Allen

Ralph "Kidd" Hofer's Missouri heritage comes alive with Don Allen's *Sho-Me* interpretation. Hofer's Golden Gloves boxing experience comes out as well. *Leo Schmidt via Tom Ivie*

since it dried so fast and didn't result in the smoothest paint job. However, I was able to get some artist's brushes and turpentine which helped, though lacquer tore the brushes up.

"I pulled many of my designs out of my head and still tried to have a little decorum—the bomber squadrons

Capt. William Smith flew *Little Butch*—the cowling is held by a smiling Don Allen as it is reinstalled on the fighter. *Leo Schmidt via Tom Ivie*

The original Don Allen color workup for 4th FG ace Ralph "Kidd" Hofer's *Sho-Me.* This art was also used on Hofer's *Salem Representative. Don Allen*

One of Don Allen's two favorite creations was *Miss Dallas,* a P–47 he crewed for Vic France. Originally painted on two Thunderbolts in succession, it was rendered a third time on France's Mustang, seen here with France in the cockpit. *Leo Schmidt via Tom Ivie*

had some pretty bad nudes. It depended on the CO of the outfit. I never had any flak from anyone since I tried to have my girls sexy but at least covered. When some asked for a complete nude, I told them I just didn't want to do it. Steve Pisanos's *Miss Plainfield* was draped in a filmy cloth.

"I didn't ever copy any of the Vargas or Petty art, though they were an inspiration. I felt a little reluctant to paint *Iron Ass*, even though it was a whimsical favorite of the crews. *Turnip Termite* didn't seem to lend itself to a wartype character so it was a challenge and I did several cartoon characters. I had an anatomy book and one I bought in London on animals. I worked several illustrations up on newsprint, though I don't know where the paint came from."

Allen continued: "Most pilots had a basic idea of what they wanted and a name to go with it in most cases. I would make a small sketch, usually in black pencil but occasionally in color. Once the sketch was approved I'd scale it up directly on the plane. Somewhere along the way I established eight pounds Sterling (about $35) as the price for a paint job on a plane, five pounds if just lettering. A few times I got a bottle of whiskey as payment but since I wasn't much of a drinker, I'd usually pass it along to a buddy. I also painted leather patches with the 4th Fighter Group's fighting eagle emblem and I got about three pounds for them but I was always way behind on getting them done.

Upper left
The color workup for Vic France's Thunderbolt *Miss Dallas*. Don Allen

Don Allen recalls that the art for Lt. Robert Dickmeyer's *Jan* was based on a photo. *Leo Schmidt via Tom Ivie*

92

"Where I found the time to do all this and still crew an airplane I don't know, but somehow it got done. I was offered the job of official squadron painter but that meant doing all of the code letters and nose and tail bands on the new kites. I said no thanks, I prefer to stay on the flight line."

In reflecting on the love pilots had for his creations, Allen said: "The paintings add individuality to a plane. After all, there were thousands of each

Though Don Allen was a bit reluctant to paint *Iron Ass* for Lt. Col. Jack Oberhansly, it was a favorite with squadron personnel such as Leo Schmidt who poses with it here. *Leo Schmidt via Tom Ivie*

Sweet Arlene was painted by Allen for Lt. Arthur Bowers based on a photo of the pilot's wife. *Don Allen*

type distinguished only by serial numbers and code letters. In many cases the painting had a special meaning to the pilot and it served to keep his spirits up—after all, they were in a mighty rough business. Girls were by far the favorite subject for illustration because there weren't very many near the area where they worked and certainly none that would match the idealism drawn into the Petty and Vargas girls."

After the war Allen joined Ad Art Studio in Cleveland as a commercial artist at $50 a week and stayed on, ending up as president.

Arthur De Costa, *355th Fighter Group*

As with so many who served during World War II, Art De Costa was drafted into the Army just after Pearl Harbor. Unlike so many, he wanted to go to cooks and bakers school, a job seldom sought. After graduation, he got his wish without delay and was assigned to the 355th Fighter Group as a cook. Apparently he had real talent; due to his being considered an exceptional cook, he was assigned to the officer's mess.

Though De Costa had no formal art training before being drafted, he had a knack for sketching and artistic creation. After arriving in England with the group, he painted the first of what became a famous series of feminine angels in a mural decorating the officer's club, then started a series of portraits for pilots. When *Time-Life* painter Tom Lea arrived at Steeple Morden to paint life on a fighter station, De Costa "learned quite a bit watching him over the shoulder—he worked in water color and I worked in oil. I observed how he went about setting up the model for a portrait, which I had never seen anyone do before."

When Lea saw De Costa's work he recommended De Costa be put in Special Services and be given a studio to become the unit's full-time artist. In what may have been a unique move on the AAF's part, De Costa was given just what Lea suggested, spending the remainder of the war being paid as an artist.

As De Costa recalled, "I specialized in portraits, which I enjoyed doing very much, particularly formal military portraits. The mural decorations kept on afterwards," and they outlasted the war when squatters settled at Steeple Morden's old buildings and left the paintings intact as a form of decoration.

Unlike many other nose artists, De Costa "did not sketch beforehand. I would usually work right on the surface by blocking in with charcoal, then sort of wipe it away so I could barely see it, then go right in with thin oil paint. I didn't really know anything about solvents and I sometimes used 100 octane fuel.

"I didn't do any nose art until we were in England. In Philadelphia, before shipping out, the only things I worked on involved drawings like those for the 358th Fighter Squadron insignia. The idea for the winged cherub came from Capt. Raymond C. Myers, the squadron CO.

"The nose art was a carryover from my painting individual mascots

De Costa works on his well-known 355th Officer's Club mural of a P-47 pilot's angelic vision. According to 355th FG historian Bill Marshall, "De Costa's trail is everywhere in the officer's club [at Steeple Morden]." *Bill Marshall*

Art De Costa's murals at Steeple Morden were legendary. Here, De Costa (left) discusses one of them with pilot Reed Butler. *Lee Mendenhall via Bill Marshall*

on pilots' leather jackets. It would start with some little thing they thought they wanted and then I started painting on the cowlings. My system for getting the most brilliant transparent color was to make my drawing on newspaper as a stencil. Then I'd cut it out, put the outer portion up on the plane and spray the cowling with white lacquer. The paper was then pulled away, leaving the white background silhouette which I would paint on rather than straight onto the olive drab camouflage paint. That helped a lot—like today's modern gesso background.

"I think my first piece of nose art was Capt. Henry Kucheman's *Miss Behave*. I liked him a lot and wanted to do something he would be pleased with. That's when I devised this white

Walter J. Koraleski's *Miss Thunder* was another of De Costa's Thunderbolt renderings. *Bill Marshall*

lacquer method, then using oil paint mixed with varnish for the actual art. I had a box of paints from doing portraits that I carried with me everywhere—I had a good number of colors. Being stationed near Cambridge there was an art store where I could buy pigments and oil so I used real artist's materials, with the exception of 100 octane gas."

De Costa was one of the more fortunate wartime nose artists in being based at a fine station facility near a major city and having a military job description of artist. "I just did nose art, portraits, and these things as a part of my job on Special Services. I got no extra pay. I also painted numerous flying personnel and brass at the Fighter Wing headquarters in Saffron Walden, the stands for the local band, decorations for several dances, and things like that.

"I would guess I did around twenty pieces of nose art; I think all on P–47s. The P–51s tended to have smaller logos and I don't recall doing any. I did a rat in a Zoot Suit for Claiborne 'Zoot' Kinnard but I don't think we used it because it wasn't appropriate to Colonel Kinnard's command position. When the 2nd Scouting Force was formed, I painted their Indian-above-the-clouds logo. Actually, several things come to mind—a cockroach for 'Rocky' Roach, Charles Rosenblatt's *Bugs Bunny*, a female figure with bat's wings for someone in the 357th Squadron, I think.

"All of my figures were out of my head, inspired by the *Esquire* drawings—I was always very interested in classic art and use of the nude figure. I tried to incorporate that into my art in good taste."

After the war De Costa used the GI Bill to attend the Pennsylvania Academy of Fine Arts, studied mural

painting, and became a full-time artist due to the inspiration of his very successful wartime art and portrait painting. He got a few jobs as an illustrator while still a student, then launched his postgraduate career by providing artwork for medical journals. Recognition of De Costa's exceptional talent was crowned by his appointment as a member of the Pennsylvania Academy of Fine Arts' faculty, a position he still holds.

Al G. Merkling, *20th Combat Mapping Squadron*

"Art was my life," recalled Al Merkling. "As long as I can remember, even when very young in

Art De Costa's best-known piece of nose art, *Miss Behave,* was painted on 355th FG pilot Henry B. Kucheman, Jr.'s P–47 *Lil Lo.* The artist's classical training is evident in his carefully rendered figures. *Larry Davis*

Al Merkling's artistic output for the 20th CMS was breathtaking in scope, quality, and size. All of these Liberators pictured were camera-carrying F-7 photo versions of the famous bomber. The early aircraft were delivered painted overall in the flat blue characteristic of photo recce aircraft, but later the paint was stripped off the aircraft in favor of natural metal. *Under Exposed!* was flown by George P. Rives. *Al Merkling and USAAF via Steve Birdsall*

Al Merkling's nose art for *Cherokee Strip,* a 20th CMS F-7 Liberator. *Al Merkling and USAAF via Steve Birdsall*

school, I had a knack for quick-sketching people." Born and raised in Philadelphia, he worked his way through school by sketching tourists on Atlantic City's Boardwalk. "I'd sketch as they walked by, then run up to them with their portraits. I had a mat on which I'd put a dollar bill and a few quarters as bait, but most people just gave dimes or nickels. Still, I was fast and made a good living."

After making a sketch of toy manufacturer Spencer D. Embree in 1937, he got a job as an illustrator, but soon moved up to designing toys. Some of his better sellers involved art games which enabled children to draw cartoons and create pictures while having fun in the process. Merkling still managed to moonlight by sketching and painting portraits in the parks of Elizabeth and Union, New Jersey. "I went to flea markets and often was called upon to do illustrating for churches and civic groups."

By 1942 Merkling was employed by Uncle Sam. "I kept up the work in the Army and all during my stay in the States I would be sketching fellas in the barracks. I got a reputation for being an artist and even started a mural in the mess hall at Colorado Springs, but then we were shipped out. I was assigned as a lab technician—I hated working in dark rooms and inside, especially after we got to the South Pacific."

Merkling's unit was unique in many ways since it was a photographic mapping squadron flying F-7s, the recce version of the B-24 Liberator bomber. Upon initiating operations out of Nadzab, New Guinea, as the theater's first four-engine mapping unit, the 20th CMS settled on flying three-ship formations without fighter escort to take their pictures. The F-7s moved to

Biak, New Guinea, and pressed deep into enemy territory. On October 24, 1944, two F-7s flown by Dave Ecoff and John Wooten spotted several enemy task forces. The crews radioed information back, then brought home the detailed photos, initiating the Battle of Leyte Gulf. The 20th later moved to the Philippines before the end of hostilities.

Merkling recalled: "As we arrived in New Guinea we'd be passing revetments of airplanes with nose art—to me it was sloppy. The fellas would ask, 'Hey, Merk, could you do a better job than that?' I said, 'Oh hell yeah,' and they held me to it!" His first nose art job began when John Wooten's F-7 arrived in the theater. As co-pilot Larry Thibault recalled: "We ran into some rough air between Christmas Island and Australia, buckling a bulkhead to the rear of the trap door. We called on the radio and reported the aircraft unsafe for combat until it was fixed so they vectored us to the depot at New Caledonia for repairs before continuing on to New Guinea.

"A few days later we got to Nadzab. I suggested the name *Patched Up Piece* since the aircraft was already patched up and John Wooten agreed." In addition, someone asked for a portrait of a prostitute with particular details. Merkling remembered, "Lt. Wooten's crew approached me and any reluctance I may have had was

Upper right
Like many of Merkling's creations, *Photo Queen* depicted the 20th CMS's photo mapping mission. *Al Merkling and USAAF via Steve Birdsall*

The expansive *American Beauty* was regarded as Merkling's masterpiece. It was shot down on its 12th mission. *Al Merkling and USAAF via Steve Birdsall*

quickly dispelled when the spokesman said that each crew member, including officers, would chip in an Australian pound note ($3.26)." When Merkling was told their ship was a patched-up job, he put the two together and the art was created. "I started painting on my own time, but soon I was relieved from my photo lab duties, which I found boring, and spent full time—16 hours some days—painting the planes, signs, characters, whatever was needed. *Patched Up Piece* was one of the first planes to have the blue drab paint removed and during the process the fellas, being inexperienced and careless, also removed part of the painting. As a result, the ship really became a patched up piece. When people saw what I was doing, that first job got me a lot of orders."

He recalled painting nose art on twelve Liberators, an A-20 and two C-47s, usually working on several at a time when they were between missions. "The ideas were mainly my own—pilots and crews would suggest the theme sometimes—but mostly I would work something out, based on the pilot's, or crew's, hometown and/or personal references." Though he normally sketched the art onto the metal with a lumberman's pencil, he remembered using "anything I could find for the actual art—house paint, shellac, oil mixed with gasoline— applied with a cut down house painter's brush or whatever else I could find. The temperature was

Upper left
Patched Up Piece was so named because the F-7 was damaged and subsequently repaired while being ferried to the combat zone. *Al Merkling and USAAF via Steve Birdsall*

Another expansive Merkling creation was *The Wango Wango Bird. Al Merkling and USAAF via Steve Birdsall*

usually up in the 90s and 100s so as soon as I put the paint on, it baked right on. The photo recce blue camouflaged surface was so hot, at times the paint would sizzle. I couldn't touch the skin so I had to rest my hand on a support.

"When the camouflage was stripped off the aircraft later and they were bare aluminum it was easier since the heat was reflected. As a guard against excessive defacement of the main figure during the remaining paint removal jobs, a solid circle of color [as with *Under Exposed!*] or a background [*The Rip Snorter*] was painted in. The circle became controversial as some thought it would

make a splendid target for the enemy to shoot at—fortunately, this never happened."

Being in a photo outfit, Merkling had less trouble getting paint than food. When the 20th was on Okinawa, Charlie Kemski, a line mechanic, became one of his major supply sources, acquiring a reputation for midnight requisitions. He traded photo work for the specific paint colors Merkling required.

"I didn't use calendars or photos—all of the art came out of my head. Pay? I got a lot of beer. The crew wanting the art would get a couple cases of beer or follow the Wooten crew example and chip in an

Australian pound each so I got anywhere from $30 to $100 depending on what the officers would throw in," said Merkling.

David W. Ecoff's *St. Louis Blues* was Merkling's second Liberator painting. Ecoff remembered he "came up with the name since I was constantly humming the song to my crew while on combat missions but they were unhappy because I would not have a nude broad on the nose art. The reason was I could not send a picture of my plane home to my

Merkling painted *Little Joe* for squadron commander Joseph Davis' Liberator. *Al Merkling and USAAF via Steve Birdsall*

Al Merkling well on his way toward finishing George P. Rives' F-7A *Under Exposed!*. The aircraft was painted overall flat blue. *USAAF via Steve Birdsall*

parents." In the States during training his B–24D had the name *St. Louis Woman* lettered on the side with no art and his mother balked at that, asking him to change it to *St. Louis Lady* for a less worldly connotation.

As Merkling recalled, "Dave came to me with his problem. On learning that St. Louis was his home, I suggested the skyline of his city painted in shades of blue with the name of the famous blues song. He said, 'Mother will love it,' so I recalled the skyline as best I could, put a steamboat on the river and created my idea of the city."

Reactions to Merkling's art were always enthusiastic, though at times unpredictable. While working on George P. Rives's F–7A *Under Exposed!*, he was in the process of picking up the paint pots and brushes when a jeep load of GIs pulled up. One quickly climbed on an oil drum and kissed the exposed behind while another snapped his picture, mentioning something about paying off a betting debt. Merkling still gets a kick out of the experience: "Somewhere, in some veteran's album, is a priceless photo of a GI kissing the derriere of *Under Exposed!*"

Hangover Haven was one of the fabulous creations of 20th CMS nose artist Al Merkling. This unit flew the F–7 photo version of the B–24 across the Pacific.
Jacques Young

Squadron commander Joseph Davis' Liberator was named *Little Joe* with a pair of dice, each showing two—when someone rolled a four it was called little joe. Merkling was particularly anxious about this one so "I let my imagination run wild. Everyone was pleased except the crew chief, whose Christian name was also Joe. He was appeased when 'Big Joe' or 'Joe II' or something like that was lettered below the cloud on the lower left hand side."

While Merkling was painting Ralph Brower's *The Rip Snorter*, a colonel from a nearby outfit became a daily visitor and kibitzer. "He told me that as a farm boy he was an expert on the size and shape of the bull's genitalia and that it was clear that I was city bred. Not satisfied with my rendition, one day he took the paint brush out of my hand, painted a stroke about 12 inches in length, and said, 'This is the way it should be.' After he left I painted in a fence post which served as a fig leaf."

American Beauty is regarded by many as Merkling's masterpiece and he remembers it fondly. "This was a

One of the very few pieces of nose art Merkling did for other units, *Queen Mae* was flown by the CO of the 90th BG who had to work a deal for Merkling to be "loaned out" temporarily. Since the hallmark of Jolly Roger nose art was the presence of the unit's skull and cross bombs, Merkling came up with a unique way to insert it into the scene. *Steve Novak via Steve Birdsall*

fun thing to paint. Usually I would rough in the entire painting so the spectators would have an idea what the finished product would look like. But in this painting I first sketched in Uncle Sam's ear, then I roughed in the figure's breasts, then the stars, and so on. In other words, I jumped around, leaving the crowd puzzled and making comments such as, 'This is going to be one of those surrealistic jobs' when finished. *American Beauty* drew the biggest crowds, becoming the hit of the airstrip. The plane was shot down by the Japanese on its twelfth scouting mission. I guess some of my best works were lost, but I never thought of it that way. I lost buddies, not paintings."

Merkling returned to toy making after the war, retiring in 1971. Arthritis caught up with him by the early 1980s, leaving him unable to paint, yet in 1990 at the age of eighty-two he was still making posters and displays for various organizations as well as cloth banners for his church.

Philip S. Brinkman, *486th Bomb Group*

"I was a commercial and general all around artist prior to the war," recalled Phil Brinkman, "worked in

Phil Brinkman in the process of painting *Aries*, one of the incredible series of Zodiac B–24s in the 834th BS, 486th BG. *Mark H. Brown via USAFA*

102

Brinkman's *Virgo* and *Cancer*—Charlie Macgill's crew rode the former while the latter was flown by Harry Paynter. *Mark H. Brown via USAFA*

advertising agencies in St. Louis and Chicago—also just traveled the country and painted." After six years as an accomplished commercial artist, Brinkman was drafted into the Army Air Forces and stationed at Davis-Monthan Army Air Force Base, Arizona, in a guard squadron for 2½ years before Winfred D. Howell, commander of the 834th Bomb

Squadron, had him transferred to the 486th Bomb Group just before the unit left for England. Brinkman had painted everything around the base, including a massive Air Force mural, a pictorial history of flight, in the base recreation center.

As Brinkman discovered, "The only place an artist fits in the services seemed to be the 'Special Services'— they produced all the local papers, manuals, etc. . . . They were all square

Leo rests his arms on a bomb, showing the variety Brinkman had to come up with when painting the Zodiacs. *Mark H. Brown via USAFA*

Pilot Bill Hilfinger runs up *Leo*'s engines before takeoff. *Mark H. Brown via USAFA*

Libra was flown by Pat Foy. *Mark H. Brown via USAFA*

holes and I was round or vice versa, so I didn't fit anywhere. However, I knew if I could hold on to my paint box I could make it. So every wall I ran into I immediately sold the CO on a mural—this pursuit eliminated KP sergeants, etc. I answered only to the CO. It wasn't bad, thanks to my firm grip on the old paint box—just painted

Gemini was flown by Andy Fuller. *Mark H. Brown via USAFA*

Pilot Charlie Macgill with his *Virgo*. He reminisced, "If anyone had an easy tour, it was *Virgo*. She did take flak damage—300 holes—but I never lost an engine in a B–24 during 12 missions. I flew my last 16 missions in the B–17 and got shot up pretty bad—we did a split-S from 24,000 feet to 10,000 feet, then flew home on autopilot with two P–51s to look out for us." *J. Charles Macgill*

Pices was flown by Van Camp's crew while *Sagittarias* took Reed's crew to war. *Mark H. Brown via USAFA*

NCO clubs, officer's clubs, recreation halls, USO set-ups and everything. To be active as an artist in the military is most difficult—in my case I so happened to have a CO who had been in advertising and knew there was some value in the usage of art."

Brinkman's official job was as a draftsman in operations since there was no recognition or number for the term "artist" in the military. According to Brinkman, a "draftsman was classified as a corporal—hang over from cloth and wood frames of the First World War in which a draftsman was quite important."

Once he started to paint nose art, Brinkman found the name or subject matter was usually up to the aircraft commander. Though his female creations were admired across the Eighth Air Force, particularly the famous zodiac series, he was never singled out for censorship since he always tried to apply good taste to the effort. Of the twelve signs of the zodiac, the only one never completed was Taurus the Bull: "I started this one sign three times, then it would take off and never return. All the others always returned—about that time [August 1944] we changed to '17s and the zodiac thought was dropped. Only '24s had zodiacs."

As far as how Brinkman worked, "The painting was done with regular art brushes. Paint purchased in nearest city. Women were chosen [as the subject matter], same as most boats have female names; all military men are hard up anyhow. No fees were charged for your own squadron but could be for other squadrons, say $40 to $50."

When Sig Jensen's crew selected a Zodiac sign for their B–24, they had Phil Brinkman change the word Aquarius to the feminine *Aquaria* in order to match the stunning nose art. As Jensen recalls, "The Zodiacs all had clothing on their figures. *Aquaria* had a strapless swim suit. I had a wonderful ground crew and flying crew chief who kept the airplane flyable all the time except when we had flak damage. When we had to fly in a spare B–24 because *Aquaria* was grounded, my crew griped continuously on the mission. Surprisingly, each aircraft had its own 'feel,' and you could tell the difference." *USAAF via Steve Birdsall*

Upper right
Though Brinkman and pilot Hilfinger cannot explain it, there were two different pieces of nose art on *Leo*, one with the girl and one with the bomb. *Mark H. Brown via USAFA*

Scorpio was flown by Farrell's crew. *USAAF via Steve Birdsall*

Squadron Commander Howell and Brinkman thought up the idea of and painted the zodiac series of B-24s while the group was at Sudbury preparing for combat. When the group transitioned to B-17s, Howell decided crews could pick any form of nose art they wished, which resulted in such creations as *American Beauty,*

Phil Brinkman pauses to clean a brush as he gets close to completing *Capricorn* for Kite's crew. The name above the art has yet to be added, and the old name behind Phil Brinkman has not been painted out. *Mark H. Brown via USAFA*

Cancer is fueled up on the 834th BS line as a P-38 gets airborne. *Mark H. Brown via USAFA*

Piccadilly Lilly, Hard-T'Get (a B–24), and *Pistol Packin' Mama.*

Brinkman settled in the Miami area in 1946 and added to his list of academic credits Washington University School of Fine Arts (St. Louis), American Academy (Chicago), and Grand Central Academy (New York). His list of completed murals numbers in the hundreds across Florida to the

Caribbean, and from Yankee Stadium to the Midwest and Canada, including several Air Force bases.

Brinkman assessed his wartime activities: "I felt I had so little to offer to the war effort compared to those flying crews and those top mechanics who kept the planes flying." The men whose morale was boosted by flying one of his creations or merely getting a glimpse of one felt just the opposite.

Rusty Restuccia, *494th Bomb Group*

"When I was twelve, I was in the advertising section of my father's ice cream business doing posters," remembered Rusty Restuccia. By the time he was in high school he was winning prizes, and second place in a poster contest got him a scholarship to Massachusetts College of Art. After wanting to do billboard work, Restuccia began to lean toward portraiture in the syle of the masters. Then the war came along.

Restuccia wanted to fly and before long he found himself attached

to the 494th Bomb Group, a seasoned and experienced B–24 outfit. After assignment to the 865th Squadron

Rusty Restuccia started his nose art career in the 494th BG by creating a fierce version of Walt Disney's Pluto for the 865th Squadron. After the normal run on painting leather jackets, Restuccia enlarged it for the nose art, as seen here on one of the Group's B–24s. *USAF via NASM*

The sketch and finished product for one of Brinkman's non-Zodiac pieces of nose art. *Hard T'Get* was flown by Simmons' crew. *Phil Brinkman*

The January 1941 *Esquire* gatefold served as the inspiration for Restuccia's *Double Trouble. USAF via NASM*

Restuccia's talent was discovered when he began to transfer his fierce representations of Walt Disney's Pluto, the unit emblem, to leather jackets.

When the 494th arrived in the Pacific, Restuccia was approached to create his first nose art. He recalled: "Some of the guys came to me and said there was a Marine on the island who wanted $500 to $1,000 to do a painting. They heard one of our guys in the 494th had paid him . . . I was infuriated! I talked to several people and said let's not allow this fellow to charge prohibitive prices. Here we are fighting a war and this guy was like a parasite, digging into our pockets. We're getting shot down every day, coming back injured and they just wanted a picture, something to relate to, that brought feelings of home."

One pilot wanted a portrait of his wife on the side of his Liberator. After struggling with a postage stamp-sized wallet photo, Restuccia created a massive likeness nicknamed *Slugging Sal.* Soon the torrent of requests resulted in *Sitting Pretty, Bomb Shell, Hawaiian Dream, Innocence A'Broad, Double Trouble, The Bull, Taloa, Girl of My Dreams,* and a flood of jacket art. "I also did quite a few jackets with blood bail out chits written in different languages. This was very demanding and took many of my off hours."

Restuccia would start his nose art with a layout, then tell the crew what he needed in the way of materials to fill it in. "They would try to steal paint from the Marines. I ended up mixing colors from different kinds of beans that gave a red/yellow paste, used to

paint canoes on the island, Angon. We'd moved up from the Marshalls and Marianas to hit Truk and Peleliu. I made friends with the natives and that's how I got some of my colors. I also had a brush made from pig bristles brought to me by the natives. Most of my brushes were shaved down instrument cleaning brushes. Actually, it was simple . . . I used whatever I got my hands on. Pay? I never got a penny for this.

"I never felt worn out between flying combat [as a gunner] and painting. I enjoyed it because with each painting I was helping to shut the door on that Marine—I felt awful that in a combat area this fella was picking our pockets."

Though Restuccia won a number of college honors before enlisting, he never painted again after the war due to a series of combat injuries. His legacy, like so many others, lay in boosting the morale of his unit and helping to make wartime just a bit more tolerable.

James C. Nickloy, *36th Photo Squadron*

Always interested in art, Jim Nickloy began commercial art training but cut his career short to enlist after Pearl Harbor. As discovered by so many of his talented contemporaries, there was no category in the Army for artists so he chose photography, becoming a lab technician. By February 1944 he was on his way to the Pacific with the 36th Photo Squadron's F-5 Lightnings, attached to the 6th Photo Group, the "Blackhawks."

"In my spare time from the lab," recalled Nickloy, "I painted a lot of nose art. I don't remember them all but I painted 'Lucky Strike' on a B-24 and 'Daisy Mae.' All of us copied each other's work. I had my folks send me

The 494th BG's *Innocence A'Broad* was inspired by one of Gil Elvgren's many calendar pin-ups. *USAF via NASM*

a supply of paint brushes and oils. I also used enamels and if I couldn't find turpentine I used high octane gas from the P–38s, which often worked better than any solvent I could find. That stuff was awfully cold . . . we used to cool our beer in it."

Though Nickloy was attached to a Lightning unit, he painted the nose of only one F–5 and that was at Muskogee, Oklahoma, before shipping out. His 36th Photo Squadron efforts centered around painting jackets as well as squadron and group patches. Since "there were bombers all over the place as we hopped islands . . . word got around when I painted one, leading from one to another. I painted a hundred pieces of nose art, I reckon, working from all kinds of ideas supplied mostly by the crews themselves. I did a lot of touch-up work on nose art that started to wear off. There were a couple of times I was paid a few bucks, but I was paid most of the time to paint flight jackets, both in the States and overseas. When somebody finds out you can use a brush, they can think of all kinds of things for you to do. I was even lettering negatives in the lab."

After the war Nickloy got three years of fine arts at the Chicago Art Institute, then started working on murals and architectural design. He has never left painting, keeping up his work on water colors to the present.

Anthony L. Starcer, *91st Bomb Group*

"Those were the days," reminisced Tony Starcer before his death in 1986. "There was a feeling of comradeship, of family, of being a part of history. I would do it again in a minute." Starcer's artistic talents were discovered by accident when, after induction into the Army Air Forces, he walked into the Sheppard Field, Texas, officer's club and saw a man painting a mural. "I told him he had too much blue in the painting so he told me if I thought I could do better, then go ahead and do it." Starcer finished the mural and right off the bat started painting bombardier insignia on ashtrays. After mechanic's training he was assigned to the 91st Bomb Group.

After the 91st arrived at Bassingbourn, England, with its B–17s in late 1942, he was assigned the task of painting the large squadron code letters. This graduated to insignia and nose art, as well as the names of crewmen, their wives and girlfriends on or next to the various positions each man served. Starcer recalled his first efforts at nose art were *Dame Satan, Careful Virgin,* and *Memphis Belle.* By the time the war ended in 1945 he had put his stamp on over 130 B–17s, including such famous Forts as *General Ike, Out House Mouse, Nine O Nine,* and *Delta Rebel.*

Understanding how he managed such an output was never hard for Starcer: he worked hard because "the crews were so proud of their Flying Fortresses, they just wanted to give them names. The attachment between the men and the planes was so great the men called the planes by name, never by their call letters or serial numbers. It was a machine you fell in love with."

Even though the art seemed to be created in a torrent, "coming up with the names was no spur of the moment thing. All the airplane's crewmen

One of Jim Nickloy's better known nose art paintings was *Lucky Strike*. Though he was attached to the 36th Photo Squadron as a lab technician, most of his work showed up on B–24s stationed on the same islands. *USAF via NASM*

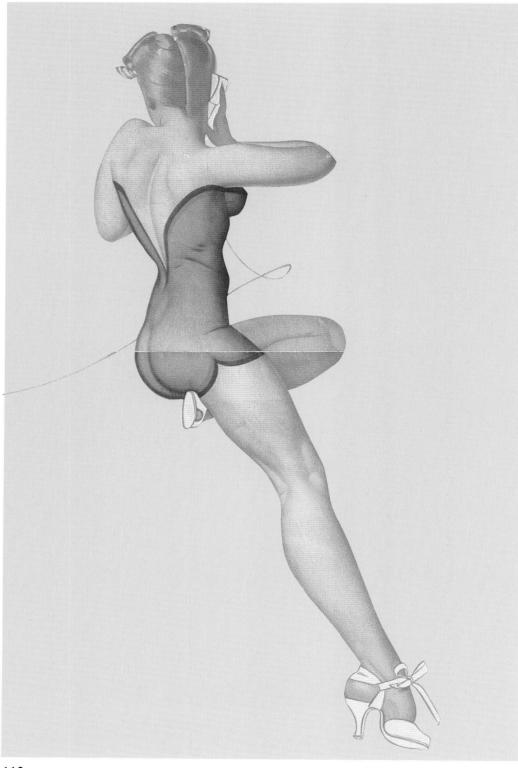

would gather together to consider a name and design. I'd meet with them and sketch something out and ask them if what I had sketched was what they had in mind," said Starcer. When final approval was reached Starcer not only painted the aircraft but usually the flight jackets of the crew as well.

All this using solely the basic colors—red, yellow, blue—backed up by black and white in the only medium he could find: house paint. He would drain off most of the oil from the top of the can, then add linseed oil to thin it out again. Painting a B–17 usually took half a day but the jackets took longer, so they left them with him. "Then they'd go off on a mission. Sometimes they didn't come back," Starcer recalled. He would put the jackets into storage and if they didn't turn up when the war ended, he'd give them to members of the plane's ground crew.

Though there were many well-known examples of Starcer's nose art, without doubt *Memphis Belle* eclipses them all as possibly the most famous combat aircraft of World War II. A Petty Girl from *Esquire* was painted on each side of the nose (blue swimsuit on the left, red swimsuit on the right) along with the bomb symbols for missions flown and swastikas for enemy aircraft downed. A yellow star above a bomb denoted 91st Group lead ship, while a red star meant she flew as wing lead B–17. Each crew member had his name on the aircraft, most adjacent to the fuselage aft entry door, the rest next to the actual duty station. In addition

The original *Esquire* Petty Girl gatefold that served as inspiration for arguably the most famous piece of bomber nose art ever created, Tony Starcer's 91st BG *Memphis Belle. Copyright Esquire Associates*

112

there were a number of women's first names at various stations—Cindy below the nose, Mom between the top turret guns, Virginia below the right waist window, Irene below the right radio window—and a large S with a tail below the left waist window.

Before leaving for England the B-17F was named after Margaret Polk, pilot Bob Morgan's fiancée, though the original idea was to name it "Little One," his pet name for her. It was changed to "Memphis Belle" after the crew saw the movie *Lady for a Night*. Hero John Wayne played Jack Morgan who was in love with Joan Blondell's character, Jenny Blake, aka Memphis Belle, which was also the name of the steamboat gambling ship in the film. With Bob Morgan's close Memphis ties the name was a natural, though, in the crew's eyes, it still stood for Margaret Polk more than Joan Blondell. When Morgan wrote to *Esquire* asking for a George Petty pose to go along with the name, the magazine sent the April 1941 gatefold and it was copied onto the aircraft by Tony Starcer. Throughout the *Belle*'s combat career from November 1942 to May 1943, Starcer kept the nose art fresh as it suffered operational wear.

After the war the *Memphis Belle* avoided the scrapper's torch, was purchased by patriotic Memphis citizens, and flown home. On display in the weather for years, she suffered quite a bit until the Memphis Belle Memorial Association, with the help of the Tennessee Air National Guard,

Upper right
The *Memphis Belle* at the end of its combat career. *Hamilton Standard via Jim Kippen*

One of Tony Starcer's numerous 91st BG creations, *Boston Bombshell,* was inspired by the *Esquire* July 1943 calendar page.

Shoo Shoo Baby being painted by Starcer in World War II.

Peace Or Bust, another inspired piece of Starcer nose art.

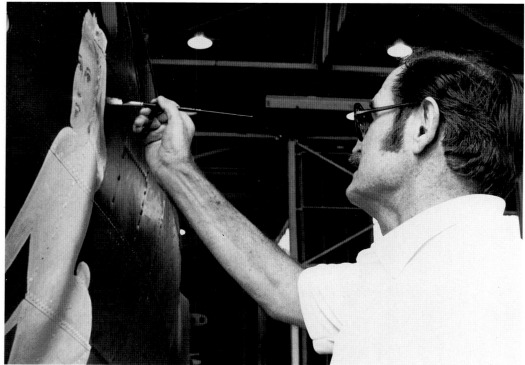

In 1981 Tony Starcer repainted the original *Shoo Shoo Baby* as it was being restored at Dover AFB, Deleware, before being transferred to the Air Force Museum. *Dover AFB Historical Center*

undertook a full refurbishing and placement under cover on Mud Island. In 1980, when the aircraft was being stripped and dismantled, Starcer's nose art came out from under the layers of paint in almost mint condition, much to the delight of all present. As crews would say during the war, you just can't keep a good girl down. Starcer died before he could repaint that famous Petty Girl back onto the *Belle* so his nephew Phil picked up the brush and proudly put her back on.

Fortunately, another 91st Bomb Group combat survivor, *Shoo Shoo Baby*, had its Varga Girl nose art and famous song name restored by Starcer in 1981 as he had originally painted it in 1944. On her twenty-second mission she lost two engines and the crew landed in Sweden after losing a third engine on short final. The Swedish government converted her to airline use and she finally ended up as a mapping and survey aircraft with the French. Spotted derelict by historian Steve Birdsall, *Shoo Shoo* was donated to the Air Force Museum in 1972, restored over several years at Dover AFB, Delaware, and flown to the museum facility in Ohio in 1988, proudly bearing Starcer's handiwork.

As the war ended Starcer gave up the brushes: "When I came out of the service the competition in art was real strong and I wanted to get married, so I just got a job and gave up art." Starcer moved up the ladder in the warehouse and distribution system of the May Company without much thought about his wartime art. In the late 1970s his notoriety resurfaced and he received a great deal of attention for his nose art creations before his passing.

Jack Gaffney, *91st Bomb Group*

Another of the 91st Group's talented nose artists, Jack Gaffney, had no formal art training other than "the usual high school art classes. I always liked to draw, especially . . . cartoons." Gaffney enlisted in October 1941, graduating the following April as a mechanic from Sheppard Field, "the only place where you could stand in mud up to your a-- on a rainy day and have sand blow in your face. After graduation I was en route with

Upper right
Nose artist Jack Gaffney takes delight in washing down the Hollywood 337 girl he painted on the back of 91st BG B-17 *The Shamrock Special. Jack Gaffney*

The Shamrock Special was unusual in having three distinct pieces of nose art, the most stunning being this girl on the right rear tail fin. As a gag, artist Gaffney put the last three digits of his home phone number beneath the much admired girl. *Jack Gaffney*

my buddies by train to Tampa, Florida. I do not remember the outfits for sure, but went through three outfits, fast enough to have them lose my shot and vaccination records each time. Believe me, if I would have had a hollow tooth, I could have bit and vaccinated every man in the outfit."

In May 1942 Gaffney was assigned to the 91st's 401st Squadron as an assistant crew chief at MacDill Field, Florida. Before shipping out, he painted his first piece of nose art, *Stinky*, for the 92nd Bomb Group during detached service in New Hampshire. As Gaffney recalled, "the crew wanted that name on the right side of the nose. I also painted a tableau of Hitler followed by Hirohito running, being chased by a huge

bomb. On the bomb were the words, 'It All Comes Back to You Now.' It was painted all in yellow paint; that's all I could scrounge up at the time."

As a crew chief in England, he ended up getting tapped to decorate at least ten B–17s. "I received no payment or remuneration of any kind," remembered Gaffney. The biggest problem was "finding time to paint and do a crew chief's job . . . it wasn't easy. There were times we had max efforts and everything that could fly went up. Sometimes we would have our planes fly six or seven missions in a week.

"I used paint I obtained or had others get from the Group paint shop. The ideas for the artwork were inspired by the crews and, like all other artists, we found pictures to aid us from magazines, etc." It usually took two or three hours to paint a

design, which was first outlined in black, then filled in during what spare time Gaffney could find.

"When I painted my second plane, *Invasion II*, I was the assistant crew chief sergeant under M/Sgt. Robert Dalton. This aircraft, piloted by Oscar O'Neill (father of actress Jennifer O'Neill), was leading the Eighth Air Force for the first ship to complete twenty-five missions when it was shot down on 17 April 1943 over Bremen on its twenty-third mission and the crew was taken prisoner." The art depicted a giant hand with a "rigid digit" middle finger and coat sleeve done in red, white, and blue stripes. During the same period, Gaffney painted *The Bad Egg* and *The Sky Wolf*.

After that Dalton and Gaffney were given LL-Z, which Gaffney named *The Shamrock Special*. As far

Unfortunately, the Hollywood 337 gal was short-lived. When *The Careful Virgin* lost its brakes, it put a prop dome straight through the stomach of Gaffney's lovely lady. The entire rear end of *The Shamrock Special* was replaced. *Jack Gaffney*

The Shamrock Special after the incredible tail transplant showing old and new rear ends. The Hollywood 337 girl dutifully

went off to the scrapyard while her two sisters on the nose kept up the war effort. *Jack Gaffney*

as he knows, this was either the only or one of the few bombers to have three distinct pieces of artwork applied to it. There was a different girl on each side of the nose, both in demure poses, but in October 1943 Gaffney painted a stunning nude on the right vertical stabilizer with "Phone Hollywood 337" beneath her hand. "The 337 was the last numbers of my home phone number in San Bernardino, California. I just put it in for the fun of it."

In November 1943, while parked outside the 401st hangar for repairs, LL-Z was rammed by, as Gaffney remembered, "ironically, B-17F *The Careful Virgin* of the 323rd Squadron. Minor damage was done to [The *Virgin*] but major damage was done to LL-Z as the 323rd plane was landing with its brakes shot out. It hit LL-Z in the elevator and vertical stabilizer section putting one of its prop domes through the Hollywood 337 girl's stomach. I was working on the reconnection of oxygen lines at the time of the accident and a voice from the blue told me to go have a smoke. I was just exiting the tail door when the other plane hit. I was thrown clear uninjured but shook up. So back to the sub-depot hangar again. This time we replaced the entire rear of LL-Z from the radio room back with a rear end from an aircraft which had its front end destroyed."

In February 1944 Gaffney was promoted to crew chief of a new B-17G, LL-H, named *Destiny's Child* by radio operator Gene Letalien. Gaffney got his inspiration for the art from the hillbilly character Uncle Rafe, the diapered kid with the long rifle. Gaffney recalls this as his favorite but unfortunately it was shot down over Berlin on its fifty-third mission with no known survivors. "That was the only plane I ever cried

over losing," he said. "It was a very sad day for me." It had never aborted, and racked up forty-four trips on the original engines; Gaffney received the Bronze Star for that. He was then assigned *Sunkist Sue*, which he decorated with his talent as well, and he painted a city limit sign on a war weary B-17 named *Los Angeles City Limits*.

After the war Gaffney worked in the retail grocery business for forty-one years, then retired and took some oil painting classes. "I really couldn't stand the sound of oil paint drying so I took some classes in watercolors and was made aware of scratch board." This led to studying under some professional artists, displaying his

work at the San Bernardino County Museum, becoming a member of several art institutes and associations and winning several art awards. That's a long way from *Stinky* and a tough war.

Nicholas H. Fingelly, *447th Bomb Group*

When Nick Fingelly was growing up he loved to draw wildlife scenes and airplane pictures as well as build model airplanes. That fascination with things aeronautical, so common among youngsters in the 1930s, led him to the Army Air Forces.

After completing his armament training in 1943, Fingelly was sent to England and joined the 709th

Nick Fingelly's *L'il Eight Ball* was his first nose art creation in the 447th BG. Based on a famous cartoon character of the day, the Fort completed 123 missions and Fingelly painted every bomb symbol on the side. *Nick Fingelly*

Squadron, 447th Bomb Group in November 1943. Due to his artistic background he was sought after for nose art. As he remembered, "I believe I painted nine or ten aircraft and this I did in my spare time." He started with *L'il Eight Ball* which was inspired by an American comic strip, then *Nazdrowie* which is Polish for To Your Good Health, and the others: *Hurry Home, The Big Ass Bird, Bugs*

Bunny, Jr., Sarah Gray, Miss Minookey, and *Sandusky Jo*.

By far his most famous creation was *A Bit O' Lace*, a much photographed B-17G. Fingelly was approached by pilot John H. Bauman with a personalized 19x4 in. sketch of the much loved Miss Lace from Milton Caniff's very popular Army strip *Male Call*. Bauman had asked Caniff if it would be OK to name a

Vega-built B-17 after the very fetching woman but, typical of the artist's wartime generosity, Caniff sent back the sketch autographed, "'A Bit of Lace' for Lt. John H. Bauman and the Gang, with my very best wishes, Milton Caniff, NY, Oct. 1944."

It took Fingelly five or six hours to finish the stunning piece of art which stretched the entire length of the Fort's nose. The bomber flew a

Fingelly's most famous aircraft was *A Bit O' Lace,* based on Milton Caniff's "Male Call" service comic strip character. Unlike so many other nose artists who based their nose art on Caniff's work, Fingelly gave full credit where it was due by reproducing the cartoonist's famous signature. *Nick Fingelly*

118

total of eighty-three missions by the time the war ended, then she was flown home, arriving in the United States on July 5, 1945. Coincidentally, Fingelly was one of the passengers. A skeleton crew flew her to South Plains, Texas, for "reclamation," and she ended up being scrapped at Kingman, Arizona.

Anne Josephine Hayward, *American Red Cross*

Men were not the only accomplished nose artists during the war. A young English girl in her early twenties, Anne Hayward (spelled Haywood in some sources) worked for the American Red Cross Aero Club for three pounds a week in order to bring some warmth to the boys of the 385th Bomb Group at Great Ashfield.

Pilot Clark B. Rollins, Jr., peers from the window of *Madam Shoo Shoo*, the B–17 he flew with Tommy Thompson. The nose art on this and many more 385th BG B-17s was painted by a wonderful young English woman named Anne Hayward (later Gordon when she married). *Clark B. Rollins, Jr.*

Annie, as she was known to the crews, was lively and vivacious enough to be well admired but her ability to paint large, well-proportioned female figures propelled her into great demand.

Living with her mother and sister Joan in a thatched cottage near the field, Hayward's primary diversion was exercising her two riding horses, a token of her prewar string of ponies and love of amateur racing. While attending an English finishing school, she was planning to go to Paris and study art but the war broke out and that was that.

When she went to work serving coffee and doughnuts at Great Ashfield, the mess officer heard about her artistic talents and asked her to decorate the mess. Then, working in the enlisted men's aero club, she set about livening things up a bit by painting women rhumba dancers on the walls. In short order she was requested to decorate the officer's club in similar fashion. So enthusiastic was the reception that, with what little spare time she had left, she was out on the ramp painting nose art for B-17s: *Dragon Lady, Thunderbird, Pregnant Portia, Shack Bunny,* and *Madame Shoo Shoo* to name a few.

By December 1943 Hayward was in such great demand that 385th Group Commander, Lt. Col. Elliot Vandevanter Jr. requested the British Ministry of Labour allow her an extension since "she has been rendering very valuable service in this Command . . . with certain essential work in lettering and painting designs on the B-17s at this station." She ended up doing a great deal of work. She recalled, "I was responsible for painting the pet names on nearly all the Great Ashfield Fortresses, the leather flying jackets of most of the crewmen, and, I suppose, nearly all the interior murals on the walls of the mess rooms." Eventually, a B-17 was named after her and it flew a record number of missions without a single engine failure.

Hayward ended up spending so much time on the flight line painting beautiful women that her immediate superiors and more sedate co-workers would remind her the primary job of the Red Cross was to serve coffee to returning combat crews. Too young to worry that the veiled resentment mattered very much, she kept painting. To keep the situation from boiling over, the base commander issued a statement saying Hayward was "a great morale builder."

Other bomb groups got wind of her talent so they began to recruit her to paint their aircraft. Once, according to 385th historian Christopher Elliott, when she took her paint pots and palette over to the 447th Bomb Group at Rattlesden, upon her return she was told, "Anne, you're a first class traitor."

After the war Hayward married to become Mrs. Anne Gordon and earned a degree in art history from Oxford University. Today she continues to paint, and recalls her close association with American bomber crews in the fondest of terms. When asked by writer Phil Cohan about current opinions that nose art is an offense against women or other groups, Hayward was quick to answer: "It's purpose was worthy, to bolster military morale in a terrible time. The members of each crew came to feel that their plane and their

Blue Champagne was another of Anne Hayward's nose art creations.

painting were somehow special and would bring them luck, a safe return from hostile skies. The art may have been frivolous at times, but it was *never* anti-social."

Leland J. Kessler, *306th Bomb Group*

Though Lee Kessler was always doing artwork and wanted to study formally before enlisting in the AAF, it was his wartime work that brought out his talent. After attending gunnery school at Las Vegas, Nevada, he was one of the first combat crewmen assigned to the 306th Bomb Group as it was forming at Wendover, Utah. Kessler started to do base portraits, and he did a B–17 painting for the CO's office wall. This led to his becoming the 368th Bomb Squadron's artist.

At this time in 1942 nose art was rather new, so only group markings and names were painted on the Forts. When the group arrived in England, Kessler was called upon to personalize the aircraft with his creative talent. "As I remember, in our outfit the pilot would consult the crew for an idea and after they came up with something they came to me and I would sketch it out. If they liked it, I would paint it and get $5 for the job . . . and that was both sides. We kid now at our reunions and I tell them how cheap they were. The sad part about we early [Eighth Air Force] groups is most of the planes at this time did not last long. They were either shot down or so badly shot up they were pirated for parts and the rest scrapped. I was one of the last originals and I was shot down on May 21, 1943." Before Kessler was shot down, he painted only seven B–17s in the group, as well as the USAAF insignia and the four squadron insignia on the ceiling of the Red Cross Club.

The best known of Kessler's bomber art was *Eager Beaver*, one of the group's early B–17Fs. She flew forty-five missions and on one of them Kessler shot down the first of five enemy fighters credited to her. During the first bombing of Germany itself on January 23, 1943, she was either the second or third plane over the target. The *Beaver* was the only original 368th Squadron Fort to be flown back to the States. It was sold surplus for $350 to Williamsport Technical Institute (later Community College) and flown one last time from Patterson Field, Ohio, to Pennsylvania. Kessler got to see her again during that time. After she was used as an instructional airframe, she was scrapped in 1952 for $175 but the nose art was cut out, saved, and hangs today at the local airport. The other six B–17s with Kessler's art were *Seelos Sleeper* which had four dwarfs carrying a bomb, *The Grim Reaper, The Avenger, Yankee Raider, Melton Pot,* and *Sons of Fury.*

At Stalag 17–B, Kessler scrounged up what materials he could and continued to draw and paint. When the American Former Prisoners of War formed after the war, Kessler designed and drew the Stalag 17–B chapter logo which has a painfully realistic wreath of barbed wire encircling a guard tower: "I guess," he recalled, "I looked at barbed wire so long I can only draw it one way."

After he came home, Kessler continued to take art courses and to work at improving, but he did not make it his career. His rendition of an encounter with Hungarian Jews from a concentration camp during the POW forced march from prison camp lay uncompleted for twenty years but was made into a limited edition print when finished. In addition, he painted the jacket art for Russell Strong's 306th Group history, *First Over Germany.*

David R. Hettema, *91st Bomb Group*

"My love of cartooning," recalled Dave Hettema, "which I have been doing 'for the fun of it' since my early school years, is still my way of expressing some humor or situation I find in life." That carried over into World War II when Hettema entered USAAF pre-flight training at Santa Ana, California, for Class 43–K.

During Primary flight training at Ryan Field in Hemet, California, he ended up contributing over 100 cartoons for the class book *Contact*. He discovered something that would last throughout his hitch: "During my military career I found that drawing cartoons was a great way to get out of some duty." After passing through Basic at Merced, California, he got his wings at Fort Sumner, New Mexico, an Advanced twin-engine school in the middle of nowhere. "I was assigned to B–17 flight training at Roswell and after some reluctance (I wanted to be a fighter pilot) I learned to appreciate and enjoy the B–17." His crew of ten picked up a brand-new B–17G to fly to the ETO for assignment to a combat group.

"Bad weather over the North Atlantic kept us grounded in New Hampshire for almost two weeks. During this time several of the crews parked nearby painted nose art on their aircraft, mostly female nudes. A story made the rounds that the CO's wife who toured the base complained to her husband that some were lewd and a disgrace to the Army Air Corps. Furthermore that he should do something about it.

"A memo appeared on the bulletin board to the effect that any B–17 displaying nude nose art would not be allowed to leave the field until the artwork was properly covered. A few days later the weather cleared and several dozen B–17s took off from the field, all those with female figures painted on their nose properly clothed and circumspect . . . until after flying through some remaining rain squalls when the water base paint washed away."

Hettema's crew was assigned to the 323rd Squadron, 91st Bomb Group at Bassingbourn and soon he "began to do some cartooning for my own amusement. But art material was scarce and of very poor quality (by 1944 the British were good at recycling many things). I remember writing to the Higgins Ink Company in the States and telling them I missed having a bottle of India ink and some pens like I had [back home]. Later I received a package with ink, pens and small brushes plus a really nice letter of encouragement and thanks for what we were doing in the ETO. Some of the brushes were used to paint the nose art for my two aircraft. Other materials (oil base paint, thinners and rags) came from the flight line maintenance crews and that's where I first heard about Tony Starcer.

"Several people suggested I should ask Tony to do my aircraft. 'He does all the aircraft here' I was told, but not knowing him I didn't ask him. Anyway, I wanted to do my own and that's the way it happened. Finding time to do the nose art was not a problem as the weather over Europe kept us down at times, or the group was 'stood down' for rest. These times we were free to do what we wanted to do."

Hettema and his crew flew several missions before being assigned their own B–17G. Working with suggestions from his men, he designed and painted *Old Battle Axe* on their OR-T. "She was a good, easy to fly aircraft," said Hettema, "and we were just getting combat tested when

While a pilot with the 91st BG, Dave Hettema preferred to create the nose art on his own aircraft using his talent as a cartoonist. This is the original color artwork that led to *Old Battle Ax* and

Super Mouse. The art survived the war because Hettema sent the "roughs" home to his fiancée (later wife) Norma who still treasures them today. *David R. Hettema*

122

operations decided to make her into a Mickey [radar bombing] ship. They gave us another new shiny B–17G," so he went back to his drawing board and came up with *Super Mouse*. The initial "roughs" went home to Hettema's fiancee Norma (whom he met in the sixth grade and married after the war) and they survive to this day in her scrapbook.

Though Hettema's crew claimed four German aircraft shot down during their thirty-five-mission tour, none were confirmed. He made up for this to some degree by getting two of

The crew of *Super Mouse* beneath their pilot's inspired nose art. Left to right, front row: Stuart C. Fitzgerald (bombardier), Glade N. Stephenson (navigator), Milton H. Russum (copilot), David R. Hettema (pilot). Left to right, back row: John C. Portner (tail gunner), Neil B. Otte (waist gunner), Robert A. Marquis (radio operator), William Lothian (top turret), Robert M. Pope (ball turret). *David R. Hettema*

Canadian nose artist Tom Dunn's No. 432 Squadron, RCAF, Halifax *Willie The Wolf*.

Tom Dunn's No. 432 Squadron Halifax *Moonlight Mermaid* carries the winged letter O which was painted on when a bomber completed twenty-five or thirty trips over enemy territory. Stars instead of bombs were used for mission symbols on this aircraft. *Russell Beach*

the ducks that seemed to like Bassingbourn's runway. "The first confirmation," said Hettema, "was routine. The duck bounced off the pilot's windshield during take-off and left its' own confirmation. Credit for the second was a bit more delayed."

Taking off for a mission to Zeitz, Germany, in November 1944, Hettema saw a duck approach head-on at twelve o'clock level, then barrel on in and disappear. When the aircraft returned, crew chief Howell Loper confirmed the second kill. He found its well-roasted carcass wedged between the cylinders of No. 1 engine. The proud aircraft commander painted two dead ducks among the mission bomb symbols on the side of *Super Mouse*.

After the war Hettema kept his skills alive and went on to become an executive with Crown Graphics in Pasadena, California.

Thomas E. Dunn, *No. 432 Squadron, RCAF*

During his high school years in the late 1930s Tom Dunn took a correspondence course in show-card writing and hand lettering. Upon graduation he went to work for a hardware store and after hours hand lettered anything he could find—small show-cards, trucks and sides of buildings—to gain experience.

Dunn joined the Royal Canadian Air Force in October 1940, then went to Brandon, Manitoba, Manning Depot for basic training and St. Thomas, Ontario, for training as an airframe mechanic. After moving through several RCAF stations in Ontario and Ottawa, he was posted overseas from Debert, Nova Scotia, in 1943 for service in England with RAF Bomber Command.

Upon arrival at No. 432 (Leaside) Squadron, RCAF near York his talent was quickly discovered; he was soon painting nose art on the unit's Handley Page Halifax bombers. When 432 converted to Avro Lancasters, Dunn continued to paint them. Though he painted between six and eight aircraft, his favorites were on Halifaxes—*Moonlight Mermaid* (letter M), *Willie the Wolf* (letter W) and a rather symbolic piece of art showing a cloud spewing forth lightning bolts that passed through the cross of Jesus Christ and proceeded to destroy the Nazi swastika. Written next to the scene was the New Testament verse Luke 3:5, "Every valley shall be filled and every mountain and hill shall be brought low," which was Jesus quoting Isaiah 40:4 from the Old Testament. He also painted Q for *Queen of Them All*, O for *Oscar the Outlaw*, and U for *Utopia*.

When Dunn agreed to do a painting, "the crew of the aircraft paid me five quid. A quid is an English slang word for a one pound note, which was worth $5 in 1944; therefore I got $25 for a painting in Canadian money." When a bomber completed twenty five "trips" over Germany, the usual custom was to paint the squadron operational crest, a winged O, on the nose.

After the war, Tom worked in sign shops in Winnipeg, Manitoba, and Toronto and Kitchener, Ontario, making sign writing and pictorial art his life's work. Retired in Kitchener, he continues to do some picture painting and carpentry as a hobby. His *Willie the Wolf* survived the scrapper's torch, as so many of its American nose art cousins, by being snipped out before the bomber was pushed into the smelter. Today it hangs on display in an officer's mess at Ottawa, Ontario.

Mike Pappas, *385th Bomb Group*

Not all budding nose artists were able to do much more than get started . . . seems there was a war that, inconveniently, kept getting in the way. Mike Pappas remembered his short lived career.

"As I recall, some of the crew of a brand new B-17G, 42-97275, were walking behind us on our way to the mess hall [at Great Ashfield]. Members of the 551st Squadron (I was with the 549th), they noticed my crew's A-2 jackets that I had painted with our bomber's name, *Big Gas Bird*, and asked if I would paint their new bomber and jackets as well, to which I agreed.

"But, alas, their selection of a name wasn't very original; in fact, it was quite corny—*Roger the Dodger*. I tried in vain to discourage their choice in favor of something more warm and feminine. After all, who'd want to reach up and pat a guy named Roger on the ass before taking off on a combat mission! Besides, I was anxious to get involved in depicting a nudie-cutie and a suggestive name to match. That would put me right up there with a *real* nose artist named Starcer. But that was not to be.

"Shortly after I did the job for them, my own crew was shot down over Munster while I was hospitalized, leaving me an orphan. I was originally a tail gunner, but soon became checked out as a togglier, and started flying again with crews whose own bombardiers had become casualties.

"On Friday, October 6, 1944, I was assigned to fly with Bill Leverett's crew of the 551st, and they had been assigned to fly *Roger the Dodger*, whose own crew was off that day. So there I was, up in the nose of that shiney new ship, decorated with my art work.

"But that day marked the end for poor *Roger*, along with the twelve other bombers in that formation. We were hit by a swarm of Fw 190s over the target, Berlin, and we all went down in flames, despite a heavy escort of close to 400 Mustangs! So that was the tragic end for *Roger* and my art work—all for naught."

As they used to say during the war, "Brother it was rough in the ETO."

Chapter 5

Timeless Beauties

The Elvgren, Petty and Vargas Pinups

When George Petty, Alberto Vargas, Gil Elvgren, and other talented artists created their stunning girls, no doubt these men had no idea how far their talent would reach. Not only would it dominate World War II nose art, but it would travel across the decades to the present and find itself being applied to modern military aircraft.

Each of these men had, as one would expect, a love of the feminine form. When George Petty sat down to create his almost aerodynamically sleek girls, he used live models, particularly his daughter, whose facial features can be recognized in almost every painting. Though the *Esquire* Petty Girl was famous in her own right, Petty was just as well known for his long association with Jantzen since he painted most of their swimwear ads using the same airbrush techniques.

When Alberto Vargas immigrated from Peru and started to walk the streets of New York, he was smitten with what he considered to be the most beautiful women he had ever

seen. He decided to devote himself to painting them, which lead to contracts with the Ziegfeld Follies and several

movie studios. His excellent portraits of 1930s Hollywood movie stars opened the door to *Esquire* where the

One of Gil Elvgren's many inspiring pin-ups. *Charles Martignette*

A George Petty gatefold from *Esquire.* Petty was the magazine's main artist

before America entered the war. *Copyright Esquire Associates*

OVER EXPOSURE

Another war couldn't keep George Petty's art down nor could it suppress this tribute to the most famous bomber of World War II. Maj. Buddy Jones' 355th TFW F–105D *Memphis Belle II* was flown in combat over Vietnam through 1970. *Mike Herbert via Cohen and Farmer*

Left, below and next page

No less famous to serving GIs were Gillette Elvgren's Brown & Bigelow Calendar Co. pin-ups. Each of these wartime paintings served as inspiration for an extensive body of nose art. *Charles Martignette*

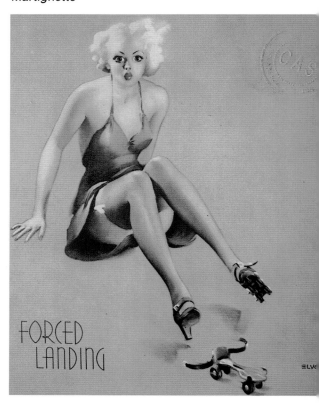

FORCED LANDING

magazine dropped the *s* from his name and created the Varga Girl.

Though Vargas used his wife and several women as live models, his imagination was responsible for most of his work. He would sketch extensively until he came up with what he had envisioned. In the early 1960s Vargas began his long association with *Playboy* magazine, creating idealized women as he had in the 1940s. Throughout his career, as with most pin-up artists, Vargas relied heavily on painting magazine ads for several companies, including Jantzen, to pay for the basic necessities of life.

Gil Elvgren was famous in his own right for painting the soft, warm Coca-Cola ads of the 1940s and 1950s. He never used live subjects per se, but would take pictures of models in various poses he had in mind, then paint from the photos. His series of popular pin-up calendars across several decades are immediately recognizable to anyone who used to visit car parts stores or blue-collar repair shops.

Interestingly enough, for all the sexual fantasy these three men seemed to create, each was married and devoted to one woman throughout their lives. With happy families and obvious commitment to their mates, they were about as normal as the local accountant. The furor surrounding their fictitious women, which every man overseas longed for, was a source of amusement, particularly when some had the boldness to ask what it was like to be surrounded by all those beauties. Quite simply, they didn't give it much thought.

Let's take a trip across fifty years and watch the timeless beauty these men created grace the rapidly evolving machines of military aviation.

129

Alberto Vargas remained the favorite artist
to copy for aircrews around the world.
This *Esquire* September 1943 calendar
page was copied onto countless aircraft.
Copyright Esquire Associates via Charles
Martignette

The June 1943 Varga Girl *Esquire* calendar page went through numerous nose art interpretations right up to the present, as seen on *Classy Chassis,* a 410th Bomb Wing B-52H at K. I. Sawyer AFB, Michigan, in 1990. *Copyright Esquire Associates via Charles Martignette; Brian C. Rogers*

This page and following page
Vargas' April 1943 *Esquire* gatefold
spanned the generations to inspire a new
group of air and ground crew. The B-52
Night Mission II was directly inspired by
the 30th BG B-24 *Night Mission* which
was in turn inspired by Vargas. Lt. Winton
Newcomb's 30th BG crew had been flying

to Iwo Jima and Chichi Jima every other
day when they asked for a night mission
to ease the pressure. With great hope they
named their already well-worn B-24M
Night Mission but never got one in 42
missions. *Warren Coughlin via Steve
Birdsall; Brian C. Rogers*

The July 1943 *Esquire* Vargas gatefold was used extensively in World War II and here she appears on the rear fuselage of a B-17 with the name Eleanor under the right waist gun position. She recently showed up as the PBY and B-26 nose art *Fire Eaters* in Steven Spielberg's aviation fantasy film *Always*, a remake of the 1944 MGM film *A Guy Named Joe.*

The October 1944 *Esquire* Vargas calendar page set up a series of nose art creations in each combat theater. *Copyright Esquire Associates*

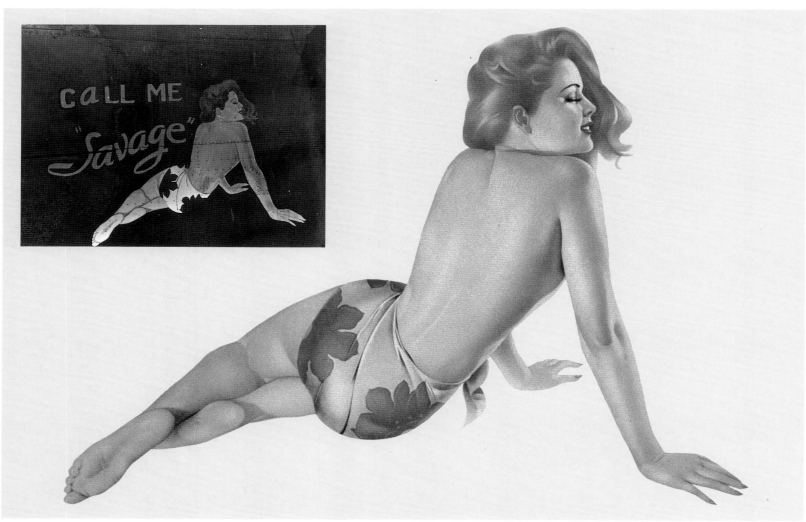

Lt. Dick Perley with 50th FG P-47 *Tondelayo,* which 313th FS nose artist Sgt. Les Schaufler created from the Vargas calendar. *Richard H. Perley*

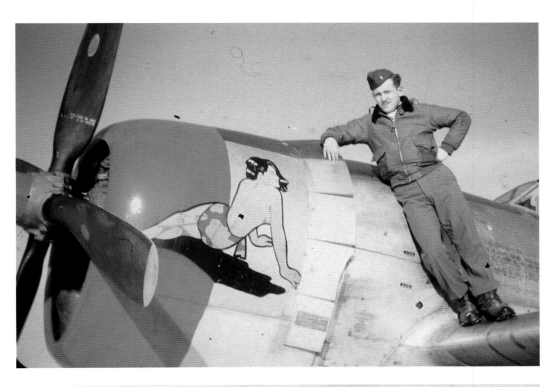

Another very popular Vargas *Esquire* inspiration came from the December 1943 gatefold, "There'll Always Be A Christmas."

Special Delivery is a 92nd BW B–52H, photographed here in 1990. *James R. Benson, Jr.*

410th BW B–52H *Diamond Girl* at K. I. Sawyer AFB, Michigan, has a few wrinkles to show its age, but the nose art is as faithful as ever to Alberto Vargas' original 1943 vision. *Brian C. Rogers*

The Vargas January 1945 *Esquire* calendar page stretched across continents and times. *Copyright Esquire Associates*

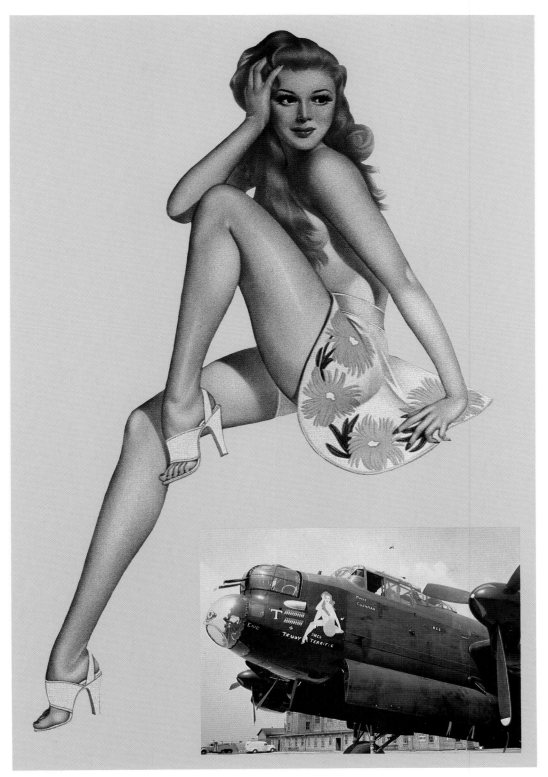

Chapter 6

Hollywood Goes to War

Nose Art Becomes an Icon

When Hollywood discovered aviation, producers wasted no time in singling out the most glamorous aspect of the recent world war—fighter pilots and the individualistic markings on their aircraft. Chivalrous knights of the air were soon swirling across the silver screen in impressively painted biplane steeds, and the first Academy Award for Best Motion Picture went to *Wings*. Howard Hughes' *Hells Angels* and a series of World War I epics followed to captivate the public.

From that point on, screen writers and producers created a pantheon of colorful markings for both the good guys and the bad guys. Often nowhere close to reality, celluloid aircraft and heraldry nevertheless gave audiences their only close-up look at what military crews flew. By the time World War II broke out, Hollywood had discovered nose art and the public

learned to call inanimate machines by name—*Mary Ann, Ruptured Duck, Piccadilly Lilly, The Impatient Virgin*, and so on. Since that time almost

every military aviation film has used some form of nose art up through the 1990s, establishing the genre as a part of national consciousness.

In addition to making films, Hollywood personalities jumped straight into the war effort with USO tours and having their likenesses made into nose art. Jane Russell was an ideal subject, as she seems to agree while looking at herself on this AAF Training Command AT-6.

The film *Wings* won the first Academy Award for Best Picture in 1929. Director William Wellman, who flew Spads in World War I, dressed up the US Army Boeing M.B.3As to look like his old mounts, even to the point of painting a

Spad tail outline. The fuselage art was a rough copy of some American fighter themes, but the number seven was actually on Wellman's wartime Spad. *Kelly AFB via Norm Taylor*

Though all of the movie studios have kept up a steady stream of military aviation films over the years, no company has done more for the real men in the services than Walt Disney Studios. Not only did studio artists and animators respond to a stream of requests for unit insignia during World War II, but the company continued to do so through the Korean and Vietnam wars and does so today. In addition, Disney cartoon characters became extremely popular subjects for nose art across the decades.

Walt Disney, a Red Cross ambulance driver during World War I, predated the next war's massive markings obsession by painting a cartoon character on the canvas of his vehicle. Most World War II crews think they were the first to paint on the back of their leather jackets, but Disney had done it twenty-five years earlier when he painted the *Croix de Guerre* on French jackets. Apparently, Disney never forgot the effect his personalized art had on morale.

In 1939, Navy VF–7 officer Burt Stanley asked Disney to design a unit insignia for the fighter squadron. Disney artists had the new badge on its way with no delay, but it was not until March 1940 that the avalanche started. Lt. E. S. Caldwell wrote to Disney and asked him to design an emblem fit for the Navy's emerging fleet of fast PT boats, nicknamed the "mosquito fleet." The mosquito riding a torpedo was sent back within days. Word of Disney's generosity quickly got around to other military units.

Several Hollywood actors went to war in uniform, among them Clark Gable who flew several missions with the Eighth AF. Though he was not assigned to a crew, he was photographed in front of a number of bombers that bore some connection to his career, among them *Delta Rebel No. 2.*

Upper left
The Jolly Rogers' (90th Bomb Group) nose artist honored Bob Hope's traveling USO troupe with *Road To Tokyo.* Hope, Jerry Colona, Frances Langford, and the others in the foreground are enjoying the result. *Will Addison*

140

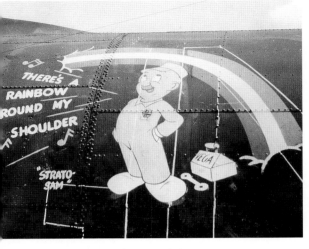

Above and upper right
As soon as Lockheed started to push PV-1 Venturas and B-17s out of its Vega plant in Burbank, some outstanding art appeared on the aircraft before they left, particularly on the sides of the fuselages. Strato-Sam became a regular character, usually with some pithy saying against the Axis. Kid Vega soon appeared, then a host of Hollywood cartoon characters. So popular was the art that it became an institution and usually lasted through the war theaters. *Lockheed Corporation*

Soon the studio was receiving enough requests for unit insignia art from American, British, and Canadian squadrons to devote several personnel to the effort. When World War II ended over 1,200 unit insignia had been created, all at no cost to anyone but Disney. The once staid military heraldry format created during World War I was forever changed as Donald Duck, Mickey Mouse, Pluto, Dumbo, the Seven Dwarfs, and Uncle Walt's other cartoon characters showed up on leather jackets, battleships, tanks, jeeps, motorcycles, and, of course, planes. The effect on morale was measurable. When Brig. Gen. S. B. Buckner, commander of the Alaska Defense Force, received the Disney design of a seal balancing the letters

Hollywood cartoon characters were ever popular subjects for nose art. William E. Scarborough's VB-144 crew painted an angry Bugs Bunny on their PV-1 Ventura, *Shoot—You're Faded,* seen here at Tarawa in 1944. *W. E. Scarborough*

ADF, the general wrote back, "Since the arrival of the insignia all of the seals in Bering Sea have been out on the ice pack balancing Ds on their noses, sneering derisively at the polar bears, expanding their chests and cavorting merrily over being chosen to represent our defense forces."

So demanding was the effort to supply insignia that Disney assigned a five-man staff, among them Henry L. "Hank" Porter, pulled off his regular job as pencil and ink artist for Disney's Sunday comics, and 250 pound gagman Roy Williams, better known in the 1950s as the biggest Mouseketeer on TV's "Mickey Mouse Club." Where possible, the team tried to tie one of the studio's characters to the job of the military unit—bulldog to Marines, Jiminy Cricket (Pinocchio's conscience) to a chaplain unit, Flower the skunk to a chemical warfare outfit, owl to a night fighter squadron. In general, most of Disney's docile and loving characters took on a fierce countenance to fight the enemy, but they remained easily recognizable.

There were some quite famous units carrying Disney insignia, including Claire Chennault's Flying Tigers and the RAF Eagle Squadrons. At the request of China Defense Supplies in Washington, DC, Roy Williams created the Flying Tigers' original winged tiger flying through a V for victory. As Williams recalled to Wanda Cornelius and Thayne Short,

Since Lockheed's Vega terminal was set up next to the Walt Disney Studios at Burbank, it was no surprise that most of the fuselage artwork involved Disney characters saying and doing all kinds of things to win the war. *James J. Sloan via James H. Farmer*

The popularity of Walt Disney's cartoon creations was overwhelming during World War II, if nose art and squadron insignia are any measure. At Walt Disney Studios an office, with talented people like Roy Williams and Hank Porter, was devoted to creating, gratis, insignia and art for military units and crews. So popular was Mickey Mouse that he showed up on the other side as well, and was the personal emblem on Adolf Galland's Messerschmitt 109s.

Upper right
Donald Duck rolls up his sleeves for battle on this 35th FG P–39 Airacobra. *Ben Ewers*

Goofey takes delight at cursing the enemy on a No. 429 Squadron, RAF, Halifax. *Canadian EAVC*

Donald Duck being painted on a No. 409 Squadron Mosquito, August 1, 1944. The gun and light Donald carries represents the unit's night fighter mission. *Canadian EAVC*

143

When World War II ended, Hollywood kept the fires burning with a series of air epics. When Air National Guard P–47s were called upon to star in the 1948 movie *Fighter Squadron*, they were painted in some very colorful schemes, most to match the 57th Fighter Group which appeared in the wartime color documentary *Thunderbolt*. Pilot Lee Gover (second from left), a 4th Fighter Group ace, took the liberty of adding his wartime score to the side of the P–47 he flew for the movie. *Lee Gover via James H. Farmer*

Karl Malden and Efram Zimbalist, Jr., act out an early Korean War scene from *Bombers B-52* involving a well-presented

California Air National Guard F–86. *James H. Farmer*

"General Chennault gave me credit for the Flying Tiger insignia but I . . . did the original idea and rough design [while] Hank Porter drew it up." When the Tigers disbanded and the USAAF 23rd Fighter Group picked up their legacy, Williams reconfigured the cartoon tiger riding a lightning bolt. Yet again there was a metamorphosis and the tiger became the symbol for the China-Burma-India (CBI) Theater's Fourteenth Air Force. As service artists kept reinterpreting the fierce feline, numerous versions showed up in all kinds of units until it became impossible to keep track of them.

Disney's characters went far beyond the official control of the studio. Nose art and personal markings spanned the globe, testifying to the impact of this man's vision upon a generation. Lockheed Aircraft, which was a short distance from Disney's Burbank studio, clearly fell under the spell. Several employees who were also talented artists started painting cartoon characters with patriotic slogans straight onto new aircraft, particularly PV-1 Venturas, as they rolled off the assembly lines. Uncle Walt's creations were the clear favorites, though Warner Brothers cartoon stars and numerous original creations showed up, usually on fuselage sides next to the crew door.

Even with this much proliferation, the Disney influence went further through the studio artists who joined the military services, then fanned out across the various theaters of war. Studio artist McClung joined the AAF and became a fighter pilot with the 25th Squadron, 51st Fighter Group in the CBI. He designed the squadron mascot, Our Assam Dragon, as well as the 25th's P-40 tiger-shark mouths which differed from the Flying Tigers in having long saber teeth.

Ground crewman Homer G. Cozby painted many of the mouths on the aircraft, as well as the victory symbols and personal names.

From the end of World War II to the 1990s has come a steady stream of films that continue to reflect a now established icon, the named airplane carrying a dedicated crew into combat. Though most of the scripts have been predictable, even miserable, the inanimate machine with the beautiful girl or cartoon character on the side has never suffered in the eyes of the audience. Art reflects life . . . or does life reflect art?

The most classic nose art seen since World War II showed up in the 1990 film, *Memphis Belle.* Though some of it was thematic rather than a direct copy of a wartime example, the girls of Vargas and Petty were well represented. The B–25 camera ship *Dolly* carried a particularly faithful example of the February 1945 Vargas *Esquire* gatefold.

Korean War nose art on 452nd BG B–26C
Miss Minooki. Walter M. Given III

146

Chapter 7

Korea to Vietnam

Almost an Historical Footnote

With the end of World War II, nose art took a nose dive and almost disappeared. There was a good reason. The airplanes almost disappeared. The United States wasted little time in smelting down what was left of its 300,000 warplanes or selling them off for a few hundred dollars each. But that wasn't all there was to it. With no war, the basic need for personalized machines wound down, though it would never disappear.

The Korean War broke out in 1950 and nose art was back on the aircraft, but the times had changed. Though there were some bold examples during World War II, this war brought on a consistent flood of

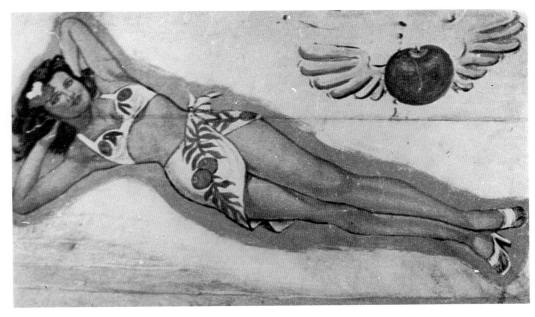

Though nose art was not as prevalent in the years following World War II, crew members would not let it die. The July 1945 Vargas *Esquire* gatefold showed up as nose art on this 35th FG F–51 Mustang with the occupation forces in Japan well after the war was over. *Barry Pattison*

As surplus Mustangs made their way into the world's air forces, indigenous nose art started to show up. The squadron badge for Sweden's CF16 made a fine example, seen here in the late 1940s. *Sture Mattsson via Leif Hellstrom*

Certainly a fitting example of nose art, C-82 *Nose For News* had the nose to match its comic imitation. *USAF via NASM*

Wild Mustangs were a natural nose art subject in the Swedish Air Force, as can be seen on this 2nd Squadron, F16, F-51

Mustang in 1948. *Stig Tullberg via Leif Hellstrom*

The 61st FS insignia on Captain Westfall's 56th FG F-80A in 1948 shows what nose art became between the wars. Except for

the flurry of art during the Korean War, this remained the case throughout the 1950s. *David W. Menard via Norm Taylor*

raunchiness, particularly in the B-29 groups. "Gone," said historian Jim Farmer, was "much of that romanticized, even modest, 'Hollywood dream girl' image made so popular during the 1940s by the Petty and Varga girls of *Esquire*. In their place we find, with increasing regularity, a more 'raunchy,' heavy-handed, blatantly sexual image which leaves very little to the imagination. Where an article of clothing or a more discreetly posed leg or arm concealed the pubic area we now more often find a new boldness among the artists of the Korean period. Correspondingly a new frankness is also now often found in the accompanying double-entendres of the period."

Nevertheless, there were still the more idealistic examples of nose art, particularly those patterned after Gil Elvgren's calendar art. The 17th Bomb Wing's B-26 Invaders, based at Pusan, South Korea, are excellent examples since virtually all of them carried nose art from Elvgren's 1952 calendar copied directly onto the aircraft.

As 17th pilot Robert C. Mikesh remembered, "Our rear echelon maintenance for both [the 3rd and 17th Wings] was done at Miho Air Base, Japan, and it was while the aircraft were at this location that [the nose art] was done. I recall it cost me $15.00 for the art work, including crew names." The result was *Monie*, named for Mikesh's wife, but with Elvgren's May 1952 calendar girl.

With the Korean War, Americans found themselves in different circumstances than the previous, somewhat pure ideological war. This would be the first of coming political wars which military men would be asked to fight but not win, for a nation somewhat apathetic or even hostile to the war. As a result, nose art, when it was allowed to be applied during the 1950s and early 1960s, began to change until a new conflict, the Vietnam War, reflected a new generation.

As Jim Farmer reflected, "Much of the personal commitment to the

When the Korean War started and military aircraft, such as this C-119 *Maggie,* were once again called to serve in combat, nose art came back on the scene in short order. *Robert C. Mikesh*

During the Korean War, Pancho Pasqualicchio's 35th Fighter Group F-51D carried a cartoon caricature of him in the aircraft plus "OL' NₐDSₒB" on the side. *Robert P. Pasqualicchio*

Vance L. "Bud" Yount aboard the USS *Sicily* with one of his squadron's colorful F4U-4 Corsairs. VMF-323, "Deathrattlers," went to war over Korea while breaking all the rules the US Navy had on not allowing nose art to be applied to any aircraft. *Vance L. Yount*

total eradication of an 'enemy,' so common during the World War II period, is found wanting in most of the aircraft combat art to come out of the post-Korean action; Vietnam will be the first war in this Nation's history to produce a totally new category of aircraft art and comment. For now many of those statements or justifications for fighting, once directed at the enemy, are squarely aimed at the people back home—the people whose interest [combat crews were] charged to protect! Vietnam is unique in the Nation's history for conditions under which such aircraft names as *The Protester's Protector, [Peace Envoy* or *The Silent Majority]* are found."

Though the war lasted, basically, from 1965 to 1973, nose art flourished for a short time, from late 1967 to late 1970. On the whole the Vietnam War was a conflict which,

Later well known as a dynamic general, Capt. Chappie James stands in front of his 18th FBW F–51D, *Nebinger,* during the Korean War. *Via Don Spry*

The Mustangs of the 18th FBW carried large shark mouths into combat over Korea. *Robert P. Pasqualicchio*

Above and right
Another high-performance propeller-driven type recalled to active duty in Korea was the Douglas Invader, now redesignated the B-26. Lt. Robert C. Mikesh flew *Monie,* named for his wife Ramona, with the 37th BS, 17th BG out of Pusan, Korea, in 1952. *Robert C. Mikesh*

The dog-eared Gil Elvgren May 1952 calendar inspiration for Mikesh's nose art remains in his possession to this day. *Robert C. Mikesh*

Little Joe Rodgers runs up his 36th FIS F-51D Mustang, *Buckeye Blitz VI,* on an airfield in Korea. The "Flying Fiend" squadron insignia makes a good piece of nose art. *William J. O'Donnell*

151

strictly speaking, did not allow one pilot or crew chief per airplane due to the limited number of machines per unit. Nevertheless, the urge to personalize war machines could not be suppressed, even when it was against regulations.

During Gen. William Momyer's 1966 to 1968 tenure as commander of the Seventh Air Force in Southeast Asia (SEA) he was adamant that nose art interfered with camouflage; it

When the 452nd BG (later redesignated the 17th Bomb Wing) arrived in Korea to fly B-26s in some of the toughest day and night interdiction missions of the war, personnel wasted no time in using the popular pin-up calendars of the day as inspirations for a striking series of nose art creations. The 452nd's Invaders at Pusan in 1952 were painted by a Japanese artist while in rework in Japan. The art of Robert Patterson, Michael, Eddie Chan, and Ren Wicks transferred from the 1952 *Esquire* calendar is not hard to spot on the nose art of many of their B-26s. The October pin-up appeared as *Sweet Miss Lillian. Copyright Esquire Associates, Robert C. Mikesh*

would not be tolerated. When the first F-4Es deployed to Southeast Asia in 1968 to fly with the 388th Tactical Fighter Wing, they had beautiful shark mouths painted on the noses. Momyer was furious, and the mouths were removed, though they kept popping up again. Orders like this only tended to make combat theater personnel more innovative.

This was particularly the case with the 355th Tactical Fighter Wing's F-105 Thunderchiefs. The Wing managed to have individual aircraft assigned to pilots, resulting in some excellent nose art, outstanding maintenance, and high morale in spite of the war's highest loss rate.

After many unofficial attempts to stop nose art, Momyer, now boss of Tactical Air Command back in the States, issued a July 1970 directive outlawing individual aircraft markings. "It seemed odd to us," recalled 44th TFS pilot Peter W. Brakeley, "that two-foot high white letters were required on the vertical stabilizer, but that a little artistry was frowned on the very flimsy ground that it 'detracted from the effectiveness of the camouflage.' Any fighter jock would have a sharply obscene answer for anyone who would seriously entertain such a notion. Art of any kind—in fact any attempt at self-expression—seems to arouse the most suppressive instincts of officialdom."

Crews loved personalizing these supersonic beasts. "The artwork," said Brakeley, "on any of the birds was normally done by the pilots themselves. Bernie Ellrodt's *Captain Radio* and Pepper Thomas' *Silent Majority* were almost minor pop art

The December 1952 pin-up and the nose art it inspired. *Copyright Esquire Associates, via Robert C. Mikesh*

classics. The collection of flowers and butterflies on *The Iron Butterfly* was a work of art." Names on Thunderchiefs tended to show up on or near the distinct jet intakes, generally on the left side, with artwork applied on the fuselage beneath. The four squadrons in the 355th used different color intake fields to distinguish the units: 44th TFS (tail code RE), black; 333rd TFS (RK), red; 354th TFS (RM), blue; 357th TFS (RU), yellow.

With rare exception, however, nude and semi-nude pin-ups did not reappear. Dennis M. Weaver, who flew a 355th Wing Thud named *Quantum Mechanic*, thought about it but had a tough time answering: "I can't really say; I know of no Thud so painted. Perhaps an increase in the overall educational level of the pilots (most [had] college degrees, many M.A.s, some even Ph.D.s), not to mention an average age somewhere around 32. Many F–105s were named after wives and sweethearts, and who wants to show them off?"

As Jim Farmer thought about Weaver's statement, he noted "a significant portion of the individual

The September 1952 pin-up was painted on the nose of the 34th BS B–26 *Dream*

Girl. Copyright Esquire Associates, Robert C. Mikesh

'blue art' of WW II's famed Bomber Command was decided upon democratically by a vote of the bomber crew itself. If the aircraft was, for example, a B-17, six of its crew of ten were non-commissioned. Most or all of the crew were probably single draftees, not yet twenty-five, and by today's standards with a relatively lower educational level. This suggests that, as maturity, educational level, and the professionalism of the pilot and crew rises, the incidence of the more erotic individual aircraft marking declines."

Overall, however, as with previous wars, F-105 nose art reflected the times. Girls still accounted for a significant amount—*Sexy Shiela, Big Sal, Suzi Baby, Daisy Mae*. Then there were pop music and rock group themes—*Eve of*

The February 1952 Esquire pin-up by Robert Patterson. *Copyright Esquire Associates*

Lower right
Heart Breaking Kasha is a B-26 that flew with the 452nd BW out of Pusan, Republic of Korea. *Robert C. Mikesh*

Esquire's February pin-up was painted on this 452nd BG B-26 flown by Walter Given. *Walter M. Given III*

Cat Girl flew night-intruder missions over Korea with the 452nd BW. *Robert C. Mikesh*

What Shebolians was a 452nd BW B-26 Invader. *Robert C. Mikesh*

Even though 19th BG B-29 *Our Gal* was modeled after Al Moore's March 1952 *Esquire* bikini-clad calendar pin-up, nose artist Sgt. Richard A. Thompson painted a nude. Shortly thereafter he was told in no uncertain terms to put the bathing suit back on, which he is doing here in October 1950. Apparently, the wife of the base commander at Kadena, Okinawa, objected to the amount of nudity showing up on the aircraft and, for the most part, clothes were painted on. *J. E. Michaels, USAF via NASM*

156

No Sweat flew with the 28th BS, 19th BG in the latter half of 1950. *J. E. Michaels*

Destruction, Sugar Sugar, Jefferson Airplane, Lead Zeppelin, Good Golly Miss Molly. And nostalgia reminiscent of the great era of nose art—*Memphis Belle II, Twelve O'Clock High.* Television, movies, and comic strips all had their influence—*I Dream of Jeannie, The Frito Bandito, Have Gun Will Travel, War Wagon, Bonnie and Clyde, Schmoo's Magoo, Give 'Em 'L* from Andy Capp. So did the Thud's being in the high-risk air war over well-defended targets—*Sam Seeker, Sam Seducer, Redcheck Charlie, The Liquidator.* And, of course, disparaging monikers for the F-105 itself—*The Polish Glider, Big Bruiser, Porky Pig*—which was loved but was large, for a fighter, as was its older brother the P-47.

Ground crewman Harvey I. Cohen watched the Vietnam nose art era come to an official end in November 1970: "When [USAF Chief of Staff] Gen. [John D.] Ryan came to SEA to inspect all the installations on his final inspection tour, artwork flourished especially on the F-4 types.

As with the other Superfortress units in Korea, 19th BG nose artists had a field day with the massive aluminum canvases presented to them. In some cases, the actual World War II nose art had survived during peacetime and was left intact to serve in yet another war. *Jeff Millstein*

A 19th BG B-29 during the Korean War. *Jeff Millstein*

Capt. Sam and Ten Scents was a 19th BG B-29 that sported a skunk for each crewman. *Jeff Millstein*

During the week that he was to come all art work was removed from the sides of all aircraft, as well as command stripes. Portable paint spray units from the paint shop could be seen all over the flight line and green paint was the order of the day and night. Six months before this happened the Air Force put out the official word that they would be removed but it took a visit from [the Chief] to have them really removed. The ironic part was that he never hit the flight line on any base to inspect or talk to anyone."

Max Effort another 19th BG B-29. *Jeff Millstein*

The 19th BG's *Miss Megook* and *Lucky Dog*. J. E. Michaels

Once again, nose art was gone from the scene—but the echo remained, to return with a vengeance fifteen years later.

Tiger Lil was a 91st Strategic Recon Squadron RB-29A which flew from

Yokota, Japan, in 1952. *Mike Moffitt via Dave Menard*

Space Mistress of the 344th BS, 98th BG. *Ed Halseth via Steve Birdsall*

When the Korean War ended nose art drifted back into limbo, though colorful markings increased. This is 46th FIS commander Bill O'Donnell's F-94C at

Dover AFB, Deleware, during the 1953–55 time period. Squadron insignia served as individual art while unit colors were splashed all over. *W. J. O'Donnell*

This F-86D at Travis AFB, California, in May 1954 gives an excellent idea of fifties color coding and the normal extent of individual markings. Actual nose art was usually nonexistent. *H. W. Rued*

160

A rare exception to USAF policy in the 1950s is 97th FIS F–86D *Dennis The Menace,* with a well-executed example of the popular comic strip character. *Air Force Museum via Norm Taylor*

Though navy regulations against nose art were always in effect, there were lapses, notably during World War II. Some navy squadrons in the 1950s managed to splash color on their aircraft in the form of tail markings and shark mouths, as these VF–21 F11F Tigers show. *Peter M. Bowers*

While the rest of the air force stayed away from nose art in the 1950s, some Air National Guard units kept the practice alive. When the California ANG's 146th Fighter Wing at Van Nuys started to receive Korean War USAF F-86As, a former Eighth AF B-17 gunner, CMSgt. Michael "Jake" Jacobbauski, started to paint nose art on them according to the quirks he found in maintaining them. *Miassam Dragon* was the slowest F-86 in the Wing. *End Of The Trail* was so tired and worn out upon arrival at Van Nuys that it had already been scheduled for disposal once. *Un-Glued* had no end of minor breakdowns. *California ANG/C. B. McPherson via James H. Farmer*

Spooky always left its pilots feeling just a little bit uneasy from the strange, unexpected internal sounds the plane made in flight. And *Puddles* constantly leaked hydraulic fluid on the ramp, regardless of preventative upkeep. *California ANG/C. B. McPherson via James H. Farmer*

With the Vietnam War and men alone in combat again, nose art wasn't far behind. Army helicopter pilots started to put colorful renditions of their unit insignia on their machines, then graduated to personalized nose art. UH–1 Huey pilot 1st Lt. Ken Mosely flew *Tail Wind,* also known as *Little Annie Fannie,* with the 15th TC BN, 1st Air Cavalry, in 1968. The cartoon character from *Playboy* magazine is faithfully represented. *Via H. A. Lapa, Jr.*

The USAF's primary fighter bomber in Southeast Asia, the F–105 Thunderchief (nicknamed the Thud), was the subject for an extensive amount of personalized nose art. Maj. Donald J. Kutyna's *The Polish Glider,* attached to the 44th TFS in May 1970, reflected both the Thud's power-off

flight characteristics and the pilot's heritage. The Polish coat of arms bears the legend "Yankee Air Polak," while the small bat ahead of the name on the intake is the squadron insignia. *D. M. Weaver via James H. Farmer*

163

Upper left and above
Sittin' Pretty and *The Mad Bomber* of the
469th TFS, 388th TFW, in 1967. *James H.
Farmer*

Captain Radio Nuc' 'Em! was an
exceptionally well rendered piece of nose
art on B. Ellrodt's Thud, 44th TFS, 355th

TFW in April 1970. *Joe Short and Van
Geffen via James H. Farmer*

Orion The Hunter was a particularly
appropriate piece of nose art for this 16th
Special Ops Squadron AC–130A at Ubon,
Thailand, in May 1969. *Jay via Larry Davis*

Though the 388th TFW had to pull the shark mouths off their new F–4Es a few times to keep their superiors happy, the Wing managed to become known for the fierce faces when they entered combat from Korat, Thailand, in 1968. *USAF via Larry Davis*

Nose art on 35th TFW B–57Es began to pop up at Phan Rang, Vietnam. The Canberra had a long and arduous combat tour in Southeast Asia—by the time the 8th and 13th BS went home in September 1969, only thirty-two of the original ninety-six B–57s were left. *Via Robert C. Mikesh*

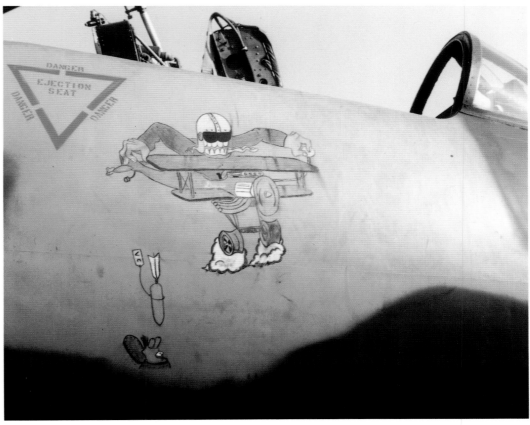

Skreemer is a KC–135A that flies with the
380th BW. Some of the nose art on
modern military aircraft is as striking and
clever as the best nose art of World War II.
Brian C. Rogers

Chapter 8

Nose Art Forever

Rebirth of the Phenomenon

With the end of the Vietnam War the moratorium on nose art seemed to be permanent, but something very strange happened. By the 1970s the US Air Force initiated Project Warrior, a servicewide directive to recall the heritage of previous history. This was not so much a study of historical lessons learned but a gut-level, almost nostalgic look back at great planes and great pilots. Papers were written, branches of the Air Force Museum were opened up at numerous bases to display vintage aircraft, and veterans of previous wars were interviewed.

Without intending to, the Air Force reopened the door to the colorful tradition of painting its aircraft in personalized marking. The 380th Bomb Wing at Plattsburgh AFB, New York, started to paint some nose art on its FB-111s and, though Strategic Air Command's Inspector General commented on it being nonregulation, everyone seemed to have a big smile when he left. Then there was the occasional B-52 going to England for the bombing competitions with some very colorful nonstandard markings.

According to B-52 pilot Brian C. Rogers, "The next chapter was tanker tail stripes, begun by the Air National Guard as early as 1978. It finally caught up with the actives in 1984." The 509th Bomb Wing at Pease AFB, New Hampshire, took an early lead in 1985 by starting to replicate nose art based on its famous World War II atomic bomb heritage. Rogers recalled that "the original guidelines were to have markings representative of the unit, locality, or base. That's generally still true today. The Eighth Air Force, then bossed by a Lieutenant General Campbell, went with the World War II tail markings on Eighth AF B-17s," and the Fifteenth Air Force followed suit. This was certainly the case with B-52s and KC-135s at Wurtsmith AFB, Michigan, as the letter K within a triangle was placed on the tail of each aircraft in honor of the original 379th Bomb Group which flew from Kimbolton, England.

Headquarters officers started referring to the glories of past history, and tacit approval was given to start duplicating World War II examples of nose art on current aircraft as a part of remembering the past. By 1988 SAC

Commander Gen. John T. Chain, Jr., decided to revise SAC Regulation 66-2 and bring nose art under official sanctions. "At first," said B-52 driver

Nose art took another long break after the Vietnam War, with some notable exceptions. When the Virginia Air National Guard began to receive their combat veteran F-105s, some still had vestiges of their nose art. Taking up the tradition in 1977, Lt. Col. Bill Harris, Capt. Jeff Wilkins and T.Sgt. "Beetle" Bailey created many colorful renderings before the Thuds were retired. *John M. Campbell*

167

Superhog was another Virginia ANG Thud. *John M. Campbell*

Upper left
Flying Anvil II refers to the Thud's anvil-like glide ratio. *John M. Campbell*

The 87th FIS had a very talented artist who was at work painting the unit's F-106s before the Vietnam War ended. *Bruce Orriss via James H. Farmer*

Big Red, an 87th FIS F-106. *Bruce Orriss via James H. Farmer*

Bones Crusher, an 87th FIS F-106. *Bruce Orriss via James H. Farmer*

Rogers, "the message change to SACR 66-2 authorized use of eight subdued colors, both for nose art and for tail stripes (on bombers). There was never any color restriction on non-camouflaged tankers.

"As the story goes, General Chain saw the reg and a couple of jets with very dark subdued nose art and said something to the effect of 'you LG guys didn't listen to what I said.' So they put out another revision to

Right
The tradition carried over when VXN–8 transitioned to RP–3A Orions, as seen at Patuxent River on *Arctic Fox,* May 1981. *Dr. Joseph G. Handelman*

El Coyote, patterned after the well-loved Warner Brothers Road Runner character, was painted on this VXN–8 NC–121K Super Constellation at NAS Patuxent River, Maryland, in April 1971. *Dr. Joseph G. Handelman*

When nose art was forced underground by service regulations, enterprising artists started another genre called door art by painting the inside of landing-gear-well doors or another door that was open on the ground yet closed in the air. *Warbird,* a 507th TFG F-4, shows its door art. *John M. Campbell*

169

Door art on a 507th TFG F-4 Phantom.
John M. Campbell

Defender Of Freedom is an ANG
Phantom. *Doug Barbier*

When nose art started to come back out in
the open, particularly among the ANG
units, some of it was outstanding, as seen
on this F-4. *Doug Barbier*

SACR 66-2 saying, basically, you can do what you want on the nose but you gotta paint 'em out for actual deployments if they are brightly colored on the camo." SAC gave the program a name, Glossy Eagle, part of an effort to spiff up the nuclear alert fleet. As the nose art began to appear, morale went straight up. Crews became attached to aircraft by name instead of number. Then the public got wind of it.

The December 5, 1988 issue of *Time* magazine ran a rather minor single-paragraph story entitled "Bimbos for Bombers," noting the comeback of World War II nose art on some thirty B-52s. The accompanying color photo showed *Night Mission II*, a rather pudgy duplication of the original Vargas art on a 30th Bomb Group Liberator, with the subheading, "Dedicated to WWII B-24M." *Time* was inundated with mail, apparently most of it negative, if the January 5, 1989 issue was any indication. One woman wrote, "As a woman who spent five years in the Air Force, I was appalled.

. . . The Air Force . . . proudly displays a half-naked woman on a bomber! Why not paint half-nude men on these planes?" Another woman responded, "If the military does not forbid this juvenile display, then I suggest that every bimbo have the face of the pilot's mother," while a third noted that as "a taxpayer, . . . I resent [these] insulting caricatures of the female gender."

A return volley showed up in the January 30 issue with positive letters from a B-52 maintenance specialist at Minot AFB, North Dakota, and an Ohio woman who was "an ex-Army nurse who served in World War II. The Air Force personnel who painted their planes way back then said their illustrations brought them luck. The artists of today need that too. So please let them continue to paint in good health and peace."

The Associated Press picked up on the story and soon the controversy was raging, with the same overtones as those of forty-five years before. "Why do they do this to us?" asked Junior Bridge, an official of the

As with numerous other military units looking for an excuse to paint their airplanes, the marines of VMFA-235 celebrated the American Bicentennial in 1976 by dressing up their F-4Js with some colorful nose art at MCAS Kaneohoe Bay, Hawaii. Unfortunately when the marine inspector general saw it, he made them remove the red paint and white stars from the radome since he said it had to interfere with the radar. The aircrew had never had a problem. *Dr. Joseph G. Handelman*

National Organization of Women in Washington, DC. "I would hope that chapter had been closed," said Mary Ruthsdaughter of the National Women's History Project.

SAC bases and HQ at Offutt AFB, Nebraska, began to get letters, some quite articulate and concerned. "The experiences of bearing, giving birth to, and nurturing a child," said a Montana woman, "have heightened my appreciation of the preciousness and especially the fragility of life. Every human being developed in the body of a woman and entered the world through the immense efforts of a woman. . . .

"To emblazon a female form on a bomber—the ultimate purpose of which is to destroy life—is not just the height of tastelessness, it is obscene. As I see it, either the irony of making a bomber female has escaped these gentlemen or they are making a deliberate gesture of contempt for the work women put into childbirth and

child rearing. I think it is high time this offensive custom be abandoned.

"If there are some in the Air Force who truly believe that for the sake of morale it is desirable to festoon bombers with a human image of some sort, I have a suggestion for them. How about using portraits of the politicians who make the decision to bomb and of the officers who implement that decision? Surely that would be equally harmless."

The controversy jumped into *Air Force Times* and the crews who were painting the art, as well as "flying" it, had a chance to respond. As it turned out, service men and women found the art to be a morale booster rather than offensive. K.I. Sawyer AFB, Michigan, nose artist S.Sgt. Kevin Hoeth said his favorite piece of work was not female but *Jolly Roger*, a pirate holding out his sword, which suited its aggressive crew. Still, he had painted *.38 Special* on a KC-135 with an excellent re-creation of a World War II Vargas

The Incredible Hulk, a perfect name for this CH-53D Sea Stallion at NAS Patuxent River, August 1978. *JEM Aviation via Larry Davis*

In the 1980s when personalized aircraft were rare, the Virginia ANG's 192nd TFG at Byrd International Airport, Richmond, Virginia, kept its tradition of nose art going with their A–7s. The variety and the quality has been exceptional. *John M. Campbell*

calendar girl. Hoeth asserted the art was based on the tanker's tail number, 0038, and was meant to signify the handgun. "It all depends on what you want to read into it. When I [put] an attractive woman on it, some people thought the name maybe [meant] the physical dimensions of the model."

To the surprise of many critics, several USAF nose artists turned out to be women. Sgt. Lee Jacobson, also from K.I. Sawyer, did not find Hoeth's Varga Girl offensive. *Tail Wind*, the first of her six paintings, was based on a picture of Marilyn Monroe with her skirt blowing up. "Personally, I thought it was cute. She had panties on," said Jacobson.

Capt. Katarina Bentler, pilot of a KC-135 named *Wizard*, said she was impressed with most of the art being created at the base. Although she did not find *.38 Special* offensive, she commented that a few other names and paintings—particularly on bombers with all-male crews—were too risque for her tastes.

Unlike World War II, no one is paid to create the present crop of nose art. Generally, maintenance crews develop a concept and the crew chief submits the proposal through the chain of command to the wing commander for approval. Rarely do flying personnel have much input, since the aircraft are too few in number to be assigned to a single crew. Since ground crews are assigned to aircraft individually by number, the machines become "theirs."

Maj. Christine Nelson, a maintenance officer at Ellsworth AFB, South Dakota, noted some very tangible effects as ground crews started to take better care of an aircraft they knew by name, especially if they were the ones to name it. The program has "infused some life," she said, on the flight lines and is "one of the few rewards we can give people who are out on the ramp for hours and hours and hours." T.Sgt. Orval Sponsel, crew chief of B-52 *SAC Mate* during its twelve-month stint on Guam, had no doubt about ownership: "This plane is my baby."

Though morale has definitely soared, swapping SAC aircraft between units so often has hampered full-scale use of nose art. In addition, the aircraft have to go through extensive depot maintenance, including a full repaint, forcing the nose art process to start all over again.

The nose art on the side of the Virginia ANG's TA-7K two-seater *Elvira* is personalized for the unit flight surgeon, Maj. David L. Hudson. Originally an Australian fighter pilot, Hudson became an MD and now lives in Richmond. A current pilot, he gets as much flight time as he can in the K model, thus the kangaroo with the Australian flag and Hudson in the rear seat with his ever-present camera and "Doc" painted on the rear door. The "Bob" in the front seat is pilot Bob Seifert. *H. A. Lapa, Jr.*

And then there are those in authority who really don't care about having it done one way or another so they lend no support to crews who want to push the state of the art. Yet, it continues to show up.

Into the 1990s nose art has crossed all barriers, showing up on fighters, transports, trainers—even the Navy has relaxed barriers to some degree. Some of the most aggressive proponents of keeping things alive are the citizen soldiers of the Air National Guard, who had kept the genre alive in the early 1970s when Vietnam combat F-105s were being turned over to Guard units.

The Virginia ANG, for example, tried to keep some of the fading art on their Thuds, but when the fighters came back from rebuild with new camouflage, a full-scale nose art

No. 419 Tactical Fighter Training Squadron, Canadian Armed Forces, has taken up its heritage by painting its F-5s with the moose unit insignia as it appeared on wartime Lancasters.

173

When the USAF started to ease the regulations on nose art in the mid 1980s, the initial reasons given centered around recalling the heritage of World War II, resulting in a rebirth of classic nose art. Some of the art, such as *Six Bitts,* had some clothing added, but on the whole modern nose artists were able to duplicate history quite accurately. B-24 nose art *Six Bitts* was duplicated on an FB-111A at Plattsburgh AFB, New York. *James R. Benson*

program was initiated to paint original work in place of the old. This resulted in some excellent art. The tradition carried over onto the unit's A-7s and will most likely continue as F-16s arrive.

The Maryland Air National Guard has been one of the most innovative units to carry nose art into the present. Under the command of Col. Bruce F. Tuxill, pilots and ground crews have been allowed to vent their imaginations and come up with a variety of nose art for the A-10s that is both original and daring.

According to Tuxill, it began during a deployment to the West

The nose art on this 2nd BW B-52G is copied from the 97th BG B-17 *Grim Reaper. Brian C. Rogers*

Virginia ANG in 1986 to supply fighter escort for the unit's C-130s. Pilot Jim Czachorowski did a pastel chalk drawing of a pin-up and named it *The Iron Maiden*, much to the delight of everyone who saw it. As Tuxill recalled, "the original enjoyed a glorious and much admired, if tragically brief, existence" due to the elements taking it off rather quickly.

The idea came up again on a deployment to Volk and Truax Fields, Wisconsin, in August 1989, "away from base," remembered pilot Tom Harritt, "and away from adult supervision I guess you might say. We decided to give it a try, so we got some samples of what we thought would be appropriate nose art. We tried it at first in chalk and it didn't seem to blow off in the slipstream. What the heck, why don't we get some water-based paint that we could wash off if it caused too much of a stink."

Czachorowski, Harritt, and others who thought they might be able to muster some artistic talent bought paint, mixed the colors, and created some of the most colorful nose art since World War II. *Iron Maiden II* was a must since the idea had started the process, so Czachorowski brought it back. *Playhog*, according to Harritt, "inspired by a popular magazine, was created by confirmed bachelorhog Czachorowski as all warthogs' dream of the playhog lifestyle. For the less artistically inclined, *Miss Piggy* depicts the Thunderbolt II itself as a work of art. [She] always seemed to show up last just before the sun went down after a hard afternoon of nose art creation." Another of Czachorowski's creations, *Cleared Hot*, "depicts a fighter pilot's party-animal counterpart with the terminology used by gunnery range officers to authorize actual weapons delivery," said Harritt.

Right
Ruptured Duck, famous as Ted Lawson's Tokyo Raid B-25, inspired a 389th BG B-24 and both were honored with an FB-111A of the 509th BW at Pease AFB, New Hampshire. *Jim Burridge*

The Other Woman, a 380th BW KC-135 at Tinker AFB on October 23, 1990, for rework maintenance. *Walker via John M. Campbell*

This KC-135Q from Beale AFB, named *Swamp Witch,* had the sole mission of refueling SR-71s. *Walker via John M. Campbell*

Another *Swamp Witch*—a KC-135R. *Walker via John M. Campbell*

Sometimes nose art remains a mystery to everyone but the crew, as is the case with *Red Devil,* a KC-135R. *Walker via John M. Campbell*

175

Mama Cas was painted by Harritt to show a woman atop a 30 mm cannon shell. The name "refers not to the departed singer but the conventional abbreviation CAS as in Close Air Support," explained Harritt. *Daring Denise*, also by Harritt, rounded out the collection and, as Tuxill recalled, "one picture is worth a thousand words. The pin-up girls were such a hit that the names of all four of them were changed many times (they were written in bright colored chalk) so that both pilots and ground crew could pose with their wives' or girlfriends' names. There was a real boost in morale.

"The uncensored results," said Tuxill, "caused quite a sensation at the time and were a source of high-spirited pride for the ground crewmen as well as the pilots for the duration of the deployment. The obvious nudity of most of the subjects was a deliberate attempt to recapture the spirit of classic World War II nose art. Fortunately, nobody took offense—quite the contrary—and, in the interests of keeping 'too much of a good thing' from spoiling the intended

Upper left
The A–10s of the 23rd TFW are the direct descendants of the 23rd FG's P–40s, which carried on the traditions of the Flying Tigers with their shark mouths. This 23rd Wing Warthog is the last production A–10 off the line and it exhibits an excellent example of door art, prevalent on the inside of step doors in all Thunderbolt II units. The tiger is a takeoff on the 23rd's official unit emblem. *Norris Graser*

A new boldness in nose art was exhibited by the Maryland Air National Guard's 175th TFG, which wanted to go beyond door art during its deployment to Wisconsin in August 1989. Pilot and nose artist Tom Harritt's *Daring Denise* definitely did that. *Alec Fushi*

The line-up of Maryland ANG A-10s at Truax Field, Wisconsin, was an eye-popping sight to people who had not seen such bold nose art before. Pilots Tom Harritt and Jim Czachorowski were responsible in large measure for painting the temporary nose art on the Warthogs. *Norris Graser*

Cleared Hot! is a Maryland ANG A-10. *Norris Graser*

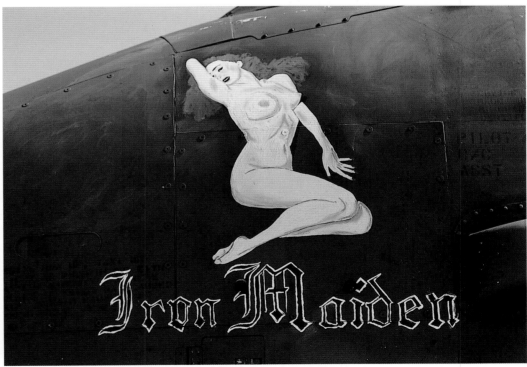

Iron Maiden is another Maryland ANG A-10. *Norris Graser*

effect, subsequent efforts would be toned down. This in itself probably repeats a historical pattern with regard to classic World War II nose art."

The tempera paint was designed to wash off so that the art could be removed before severe repercussions from higher authority set in but, as Harritt reflected, "it turned out tempera was as tough as could be . . . we even went through some misty rain a couple of times without it washing off. You have to really soak and scrub it to get it off with a brush—it comes off like plaster or mud.

"The crew chiefs were so pleased with one they sprayed some lacquer over it so it would never wash off. When they got back to Baltimore and

Left
Nose artist and 175th TFG pilot Tom Harritt looks down from the cockpit of his *Mama Cas* during the 1989 Wisconsin deployment. Note the step door art—it is the Maryland state flag. *Norris Graser*

During their 1990 Wisconsin deployment, Col. Bruce Tuxill's 175th TFG toned down the nose art, but he let the artists be as creative as before. Though words had come down from the Pentagon about the last series of paintings, there were no serious repercussions, due in large measure to the high morale the Maryland troops were experiencing over the art. *Maryland ANG/175th TFG*

were told to get it off the airplane, they had a hell of a time, using all kinds of thinner and acetone, but to this day one of the planes will have a big ghost of the silhouette until it goes through phase overhaul and gets repainted."

Though the nose art was short-lived, aviation photographers Norris Graser and Alec Fushi happened to be at Volk Field long enough to capture it on film and get it published. Reaction was immediate and there was even a set of scale model decals created. As Harritt recalled, "We really didn't know what the repercussions would be, but we left them on anyway. There was a little bit of apprehension on the part of our commanders after we got back to [Baltimore]. I understand we got a couple of calls from the Pentagon when the photos were first published but it was evidently not badly received at that level. Colonel Tuxill, to his credit, recognized there was no harm done, and it was having an overall positive effect. With a different commander I think it would have been impossible and repercussions could have been bad."

In 1990 the Maryland A-10s deployed back to Wisconsin. "It went very well and morale was high to begin with," said Harritt. "At the end of the exercise we made quite a production of painting another batch of airplanes with new nose art. Everybody got a kick out of it, even the women. No one took offense at it and we did have strict guidelines from Col. Tuxill about doing nothing obscene. We didn't see any need to do anything like that anyway. It was a formal morale/reward kind of thing at the end of our very successful ORI [operational readiness inspection]. I painted *Iron Maiden III* but my favorite has always been *Mama CAS*.

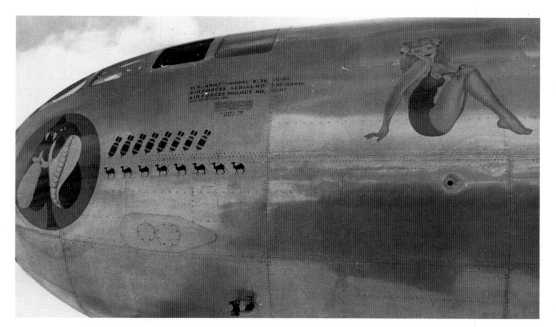

Rebel Queen, though based on a nose art T-shirt ad in a catalog, actually started with the Alberto Vargas August 1943 *Esquire* gatefold. It was used as the basis for numerous WW II nose art creations, such as this 444th BS B-29, as well as 4th FG ace Freddie Glover's P-51 of the same name. *Maryland ANG/175th TFG*

Another 175th TFG A-10, *I Want You.*
Maryland ANG/175th TFG

Left
Kawabunga of the 175th TFG is the pilot's tribute to his kids and a new generation of nose art. *Maryland ANG/175th TFG*

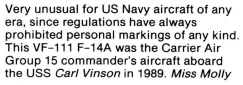

Very unusual for US Navy aircraft of any era, since regulations have always prohibited personal markings of any kind. This VF-111 F-14A was the Carrier Air Group 15 commander's aircraft aboard the USS *Carl Vinson* in 1989. *Miss Molly* was named after Molly Snead, a lifelong friend and nurse to Congressman and Mrs. Carl Vinson. Snead, a World War II navy nurse, christened the carrier in 1980. *Dr. Joseph G. Handelman*

Playhog, a cross between the A-10s nickname of Warthog and *Playboy* Magazine, was very popular with 175th TFG troops. *Maryland ANG/175th TFG*

We toned them down quite a bit." With a smile, Tuxill commented on the new *Maiden*: "A sincere effort was made by Tom to comply with my direction that depiction of pin-up style nose art be kept in good taste and that totally nude subjects not be portrayed . . . the strategically placed 'Remove Before Flight' streamer was, in this case, left in place."

Harritt painted *Rebel Queen* on Gary Wingo's A-10 using a T-shirt ad from a magazine as a pattern. Though he recognized it as a piece of real World War II nose art, he had no idea this was 4th Fighter Group ace Fred Glover's Mustang nose art. Tuxill's aircraft, *Condition Red*, was painted by maintenance control T.Sgt. Mike Montalvo. As Tuxill related, "In condition red (under attack) we stop flying, but I was determined to maintain the pace of our sortie generation. The duck's tail feathers are the artist's rather irreverent interpretation of my tactical callsign, Firebird. Since the first episode of unofficial nose art made its appearance some time ago, I directed that there be no profanity on the aircraft. The artist thoughtfully complied with my request by voluntarily censuring his own work! A gas mask and hand held radio round out the well-dressed duck."

I Want You was painted by pilot Steve Burgess on a traditional theme. *Kawabunga* was created by Frank Arnone and Jim Czachorowski, reflecting the popular culture of preadolescent kids at home. Tommy O'Sullivan's *Chainsaw* was painted by Czachorowski to reflect this popular pilot's ethnic heritage and his nickname, which happens to be Chainsaw. *Playhog* and *Miss Piggy* showed up again as well.

Having reestablished a strong tradition, modern military pilots and

American military aircraft have once again put nose art off the endangered species list. As in every era it has appeared, this most unique of art forms has gained a devoted following of air and ground crews who find something personal happens when one names cold machines meant for war. As one can see from the bombers and tankers of SAC, the variety is as diverse as the artists and crews, sometimes playful, sometimes deadly, just like it was in other wars in other times. Maybe one day future crews will look back and try to decipher the real meaning of these brief glimpses into the psyche of this indestructable art form. *Sunrise Surprise* is a B-1B from the 319th BW. *Brian C. Rogers*

The KC-135's new camouflage made it look like Orca, the killer whale, so the name of this 28th BW KC-135R fits perfectly. *Brian C. Rogers*

This KC–135A was attached to the 28th BW. *Brian C. Rogers*

Left
A 7th AREFS, 7th BW KC–135A. *Brian C. Rogers*

Lower left
Flying Ace wore "Peanuts" nose art with the 7th BW. *Brian C. Rogers*

Tankersaurus is a very appropriate piece of nose art for this aging 93rd BW KC–135A. *Brian C. Rogers*

A 920th AREFS, 379th BW KC-135A.
Brian C. Rogers

Top Off, a 920th AREFS, 379th BW
KC-135A. *Brian C. Rogers*

Right
Sod Buster, a 5th BW B-52H. *Brian C.
Rogers*

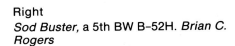

Thunder Child a B-1B attached to the
28th BW. *Brian C. Rogers*

A 28th BW EC–135G. *Brian C. Rogers*

Donald Duck is reproduced just as he was on a WW II bomber, saying *Let's Make a Deal* to the enemy on this 379th BW B–52G. *Brian C. Rogers*

crews have little doubt they will continue to carry on in the wake of some seventy-five years of what has gone before them. It may wax and wane as it always has, but, as in the past, if crews have anything to say about it, this most unique of art forms will continue—nose art forever!

Christine, a B–1B, sits at Davis-Monthan AFB. *Norris Graser*

Gremlin flew with the 37th BS, 28th BW at Ellsworth AFB. *Jim Burridge*

Right
Hoover makes light of this KC-135R, 28th AREFS, 28th BW, at Ellsworth AFB—those engines can suck up most anything. *Jim Burridge*

War Lord, a KC-10A at Westover AFB. *H. A. Lapa*

Right
Destiny Unknown, a 92nd BW B-52H, certainly brings out the reality of modern strategic flying. *James R. Benson, Jr.*

185

Metal Mistress, a 92nd BW B–52H at Fairchild AFB, has nose art based on Alberto Vargas' September 1941 *Esquire* calendar. Nothing changes but the clothes. *Robert F. Dorr*

Upper left
The remarkable nose art on *Excalibur,* a 92nd AREFS KC–135A, was painted by Sgt. Tiorgison. *James R. Benson, Jr.*

Great White is certainly appropriate for this 68th ARW KC–10A at Dover AFB. *Robert F. Dorr*

A B–1B from Plattsburgh AFB. *Robert F. Dorr*

Under Project Warrior, many of the F–16s based at Hahn, Germany, were painted with nose art. Pilot Steve Vihlen had crew chief Dave Phillips reprise the nose art from Robert S. Johnson's 56th FG P–47 *In The Mood. Steve Vihlen*

Sac Time, a 416th Bomb Wing B–52G, carries an excellent recreation of Alberto Vargas' famous World War II *Esquire* girl. The seven larger bomb symbols stand for missions flown out of Moron while the other 26 silhouettes indicate missions flown from Jedda, all during the 1991 Gulf War. *Brian C. Rogers*

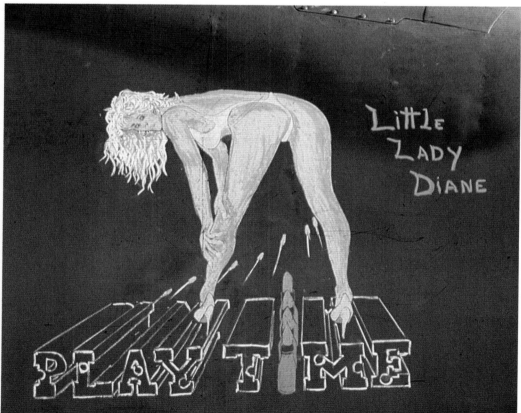

Clearly the crew of 135th AREFG KC-135 0005 took their *Ol Lightnen* into combat realizing she needed a bit of coaxing to get the most out of her aging airframe. *USAF, T/Sgt. D. S. McMichael*

Upper left
When Operation Desert Shield ended up in another real shooting war, Desert Storm, during January and February 1991, nose art flourished in spite of potential trouble with Muslim prohibitions on such displays. A 135th AREFG KC-135E from Knoxville, *High Octane Taz*, carries a good representation of Warner Brothers' Tazmanian Devil cartoon character as well as ten camel symbols for the number of combat refueling missions flown so far. The arabic symbols repeat the last four digits of the Stratotanker's serial number. *USAF Photo by T/Sgt. D. S. McMichael*

A-10 Thunderbolt II *Little Lady Diane/Play Time* was flown in combat during Desert Storm with the 23rd TFW, which also carried shark mouths on their aircraft as the unit's P-40s did in World War II. *USAF Photo by T/Sgt. William Bloszinsky*

Jester, a KC–135 with the 1701st AREFW, rode into combat with bared teeth during Operation Desert Storm in January and February 1991. *USAF, SMA. Chris Putnam*

Upper right
Panther Princess rides a GAU–8 30mm cannon into combat in February 1991 on the nose of a 23rd TFW A–10. *USAF, T/Sgt. William Bloszinsky*

A new generation of aircrew go to war during Desert Storm in February 1991 with *Stone Age Mutant Ninja Tanker,* a KC–135A of the 1701st AREFW. *USAF, SMA. Chris Putnam*

Airman James Barden, a pneudraulics system specialist from the 9th Strategic Recon Wing at Beale AFB, CA, painted each of the unit's U-2s while in the combat theater during Desert Storm. The distinctive dragon with palm tree was rendered in chalk and covered with Scotchgard for protection. *USAF, T/Sgt. Rose Reynolds*

Index